Edward Everett Hale

Easter: a collection for a hundred friends

Edward Everett Hale

Easter: a collection for a hundred friends

ISBN/EAN: 9783741196041

Manufactured in Europe, USA, Canada, Australia, Japa

Cover: Foto ©Andreas Hilbeck / pixelio.de

Manufactured and distributed by brebook publishing software (www.brebook.com)

Edward Everett Hale

Easter: a collection for a hundred friends

EASTER

A COLLECTION

FOR A

HUNDRED FRIENDS.

EDWARD E. HALE.

BOSTON:
J. STILMAN SMITH & CO.,
30 FRANKLIN STREET.
1886.

Copyright secured by
J. STILMAN SMITH & COMPANY,
1886.

Greenfield, Mass.:
Press of the H. D. Watson Printing Company.

THIS is a collection of sermons and of favorite poems, which I have made for many friends. The sermons have been preached in the South Congregational Church, at different times within the last fifteen years.

EDWARD E. HALE.

BOSTON, April, 1886.

Table of Contents.

PALM SUNDAY, Matt. xxi, 10, 11.	5
PALM SUNDAY	13
PASSION WEEK	15
THIRST	24
THE VICTORY	25
SOLACE IN SORROW	32
LIFE AND ITS ENEMIES	33
THE NEW BIRTH	41
INCREASE OF LIFE	42
THE LAW OF CHANGE	49
CONSIDER THE LILIES	50
LUTHER'S EASTER HYMN	58
EASTER	60
GOOD FROM EVIL	67
THE MIRACLE OF LIFE	68
EASTER DAY	76
THE SUN OF RIGHTEOUSNESS	79
THE FAREWELL AT AZAN	86
THE LIFE WAS THE LIGHT OF MEN	87
THE SECRET PLACE OF THE MOST HIGH	94
IMMORTAL	95
LISTENING	102
MANY HOMES	103

PALM SUNDAY.

"When he was come into Jerusalem all the city was moved, saying, ' Who is this?' And the multitude said, ' This is the prophet Jesus, of Nazareth of Galilee.' "—MATT. xxi, 10, 11.

WITH the exercises of Passion Week, the Roman Church abruptly leaps from its commemoration of forty days of fasting in the beginning of the Gospel Year, to its celebration of the end :—the week of triumph, trial and death. The latter service is far more appropriate than the former. The asceticism of a formal Lent is scarcely in place in the lengthening days of a year renewed. But of that week at Jerusalem, in which the various lines of the Saviour's life are twisted all together, in which all his prophecies of his personal life came to their fulfillment, in which that life taught its last lessons and he bade the world farewell,—of that week it is not strange that every word has been treasured, and that the world has been glad to reproduce every picture. Whether on canvas, or in song or story, or in the simple dramatic representation which calls the world to the Upper Ammergau, where simple peasants act out the scene ; these events of Passion Week come up again and again, for the world's study, its questioning, its admiration, and its tears! Little wonder. And as little, that he who hears the story told by a new narrator, or looks upon it from a new standpoint, always finds in it as it goes on, something that is new.

Jesus had already excited the anger of the coteries of priests and politicians at Jerusalem. He did not like them, they did not like him. Nothing more different from his almost festive summer life in Galilee, than the hard collisions, now with priests, now with policemen of temple courts and the streets of the city. Such a city! A petty provincial capital numbering perhaps 50,000 people, sustaining among themselves all the jealousies and intrigues of a garrison town, and at the same time those of an ecclesiastical metropolis. Magnify a hundred fold the petty squabbles of an English provincial cathedral town, and you have, I suppose, some idea of the local politics of Jerusalem. It is to be remembered that here only were the priests of the Jewish religion, here only was the temple, here were all the sacrifices. But the spirit of Judaism was now far higher and nobler than this old-fashioned butchery of oxen and sheep in worship,—though that had served well enough for the expression of faith of a simple pastoral age. The spirit of Judaism had risen to union in prayer, to instruction in the meeting-house,—it assembled congregations and preachers in every Nazareth and Capernaum of the land. The priests—inheriting their place and privilege—looked jealously at all this body of teachers, some of them men of great distinction but none of them priests. Imagine, then, with what disgust they must have looked upon a teacher like this Jesus of Nazareth who came from the ranks, a radical come-outer as they saw him, who spoke with a Galilean accent, and was followed by Galilean admirers, when he came into temple courts, to denounce and to ridicule them and their old-time butcheries. Nothing in the whole story is easier to account for, than the dislike which Jerusalem had for Jesus and his dislike for the leaders of opinion and life in Jerusalem.

The alliance of the political leaders with the church leaders at Jerusalem, was of the very closest. As long ago as the time of Herod the Great, the Herod who killed the infants at Bethlehem, he had ennobled the family of one of his many wives by making them High Priests, and this family connection again and again appears in the line of the priesthood. This family alternated, at irregular intervals, in this high office with Annas and his family. Annas himself held it for seven years, and afterward was the real director of affairs when one of his sons, or his son-in-law, was nominally in power. At the time of Jesus' death the nominal High Priest was Joseph Kaiaphas, the son-in-law of Annas, but Annas, or Hanan in the Hebrew spelling, was himself still the advising and really efficient head of the priesthood, and with th family of the Herods, which still had influence, he was on intimate terms. Archelaus, the Herod who had reigned in Jerusalem, was now deposed, and Judaea was held by Pilate as a Roman province. But another Herod, the tetrarch of Galilee, was in the city, as any other Jew might be, for the religious solemnities of the season. Between him and Pilate, as the gospel tells us, there had been some quarrel, but they made friends over the Saviour's body, and their political relationships had always placed them on the same side, the side of a dry and hard determination to maintain things as they were.

All these priests and governors had had enough and more than enough of Jesus of Nazareth. Once and again he had been in Jerusalem, driving the people wild with enthusiasm, calling away men's attention from venerable forms of worship, and saying, without hesitation, that there were ways of coming to God much nearer than these ways of altar and temple. Once and again the wounded susceptibilities of these leaders had roused them against him, to arrest him, to stone him for blasphemy, to excommunicate his followers. But, thus far, the evident popular favor had been on his side and had been too much for them. The last time he was in the neighborhood, however, the old High Priest Annas, whose nod was law, had given the word, impatiently enough, "Ye know nothing at all, if you do not see that it is better for us that this one man die, than that all of us be overturned together, and our nation destroyed, in the loosening of all ties which will come out of such heresy." Unconscious prophecy! But it was spoken with no thought of the sense we give these words! Better he should die, if things cannot otherwise be kept as they are. That was what the old High Priest meant. It was his "word of order."

It is to a city whose higher circles are thus bitter against him, that Jesus comes down again, on the day of triumph which we call Palm Sunday. The wave of enthusiasm around him is the jubilant delight of a few hundred Galileans, who are now sure that the time is come, and that Israel shall enjoy her own again. The white city below him, beyond the steep valley, covers the hard, set propriety and insulted dignity of these determined priests. These Galileans know nothing and care nothing. But Jesus knows, and he foresees the whole.

He loves Jerusalem as every child of David and of Abraham loved her. "If I forget thee, oh Jerusalem, may my right hand forget her cunning!" "Beautiful for situation, the joy of the whole earth is Mount Zion, the city of the Great King." Such were the songs they had been singing as they marched, with the enthusiasm with which to-day we sing,

"Jerusalem, my happy home,
Name ever dear to me!"

And with the same idea of a possible city of God, the home of every hallowed aspiration. But the real Jerusalem, this hot-bed of priestly intrigue and political corruption! Always its habits, methods and vices had been hateful to Jesus, and always he had condemned them. Not hard to make out that stupid, narrow dryness of the thousand-year-old little town, which was left one side of the movement of the world, and was priding itself on its traditions of the days of David. Take your picture from any place you know of fifty thousand people. Imagine such a town, half-garrison and half-cathedral, all living on the State or the Church, all satisfied that country folks are fools, indeed, that all the world, outside their own walls, are of some lower order of being. Remember of Jerusalem that its only associations of business with the outside, are when three or four times a year these people came in, in their reverent faith, to render worship which they can render nowhere outside these walls. If you care to go farther, imagine the seventy notables of such a town assembled in council, purblind in their ignorance of God's ways in the larger world, working their cause in the dark, backwards and forwards, like so many moles in the ground, sure that they and they only are the centres of creation, and that their interpretation of God, Law, Prophet and Messiahship is the only interpretation. That is the Sanhedrim or Council of 70 of the real Jerusalem, on which Jesus looked, even as the echo of the songs which described the ideal Jerusalem rang in his ears. No wonder that as he looked down on such a city he wept over it!

"Oh Jerusalem, Jerusalem, if thou hadst known in this thy day, the things which belong unto peace! But now are they hid from thine eyes!"

He had been willing to accept the loyal homage of his Galilean friends. A passage in the prophet Zechariah said, "Thy king cometh unto thee meek, and sitting on an ass," contrasting the Messiah thus with the lordly state of human royalty. Jesus accepts that figure, sends for an ass to ride upon as he leaves Martha's and Mary's home in Bethany, and in this humble state turns the brow of the Mount of Olives, and meets the throng of enthusiasts who are pouring out, in knowledge that he is coming.

It is the most beautiful as it is the easiest entrance into Jerusalem.

To this hour travelers even from the west pass round the city to enter on this side, and the general view from the Mount of Olives is that from which they derive their abiding impression of the city. The summit of that hill is half a mile from Jerusalem and completely overlooks it. The city itself from this summit appears to be a regular inclined plain, sloping gently and uniformly from west to east, or toward the observer. The walls, almost in a quadrangle, are and were white to the eye ; and the southeast corner of the quadrangle is that nearest to the eye. This is the point, which as Christ looked down, was occupied by the gorgeous temple which Herod had built on the site of Solomon's, really sheeted with silver in places, and with gilded ornaments, in the lavishness of that Eastern adornment, flashing in the sun. " Beautiful for situation," indeed ! " Joy of the whole world !" It is this spectacle, always grand and always new, which flashes on the sight of the jubilant throng of Galilean pilgrims, jubilant because for the first time the favorite whom they have tried to crown in vain, has assumed a symbol of triumph, however humble. "Fear not, daughter of Zion, thy King comes to thee." That is what he said in substance, when he sent for the ass on which he rode. Because he says this, the throng of wayfarers break palm branches from the trees, palms always emblems of immortality and victory, wave them in the air, throw them beneath his feet, and shout, " Hosanna to the King of Israel ! Hosanna to him that cometh in the name of the Lord ! Hosanna in the highest !" Yes, and the news of triumph is borne already into the city. Beneath the feet of purblind priests and outside of their musty councils there are those who have listened at the Feast of Tabernacles, nay, who have stood at the open grave of Lazarus. Easy for them to catch the signal of his approach, and they run down the streets and up the hill to meet the throng, with the same cry, " Hosanna in the highest !"

The whole city is moved, and catches up the cry. On the eve of a festival, they have nothing to do but to run and see processions, indeed, they have nothing else to do at any time. A little town like that, in the carelessness of Oriental life, would give up half its people to the welcome of the popular young leader from the North ; and the Old Line, officiating at altar, or holding forth in temple courts, would find they were quite forgotten and deserted while the pageant went on. " Ye perceive that ye prevail nothing," says one of them to another, "behold the world is gone after him." Unconscious prophecy again!"

And so the enlarging multitude sweeps into the temple courts. The mob from the city catch for the moment the impulse from the enthusiasm of the country, as mobs will. The children even are shouting, "Hosanna!" "Master," says some official to Jesus in pretended respect, "can you not silence these shouts?" "I tell you if these should hold their peace the very stones would find a voice." But the little triumph is soon over. The twilight of a short spring day comes on, and he and his go out to Bethany for rest.

The counter lesson of that triumph is told in the stormy passages of the week, in the crafty efforts to make him commit himself as a rebel, and in his denunciations of the bigotry, hypocrisy, and irreligion, of these blind leaders of the blind. The last contrast of all, is when the same mob of Jerusalem, having been seduced as the leaders of mobs knew how, to utter the other cry, shouts, "Crucify! Crucify!" where it did shout "Hosanna!" The contrasted picture is the view of Jerusalem from another Hill, as he and John and Mary look across upon it against the blackness of the angry storm, and as another procession of the daughters of Jerusalem, wringing their hands and weeping in the bitterness of their hearts, return from Calvary to the gates of the heartless city. The story of Palm Sunday is not complete without the counter story of the Friday which followed.

We may say that its warning is the warning to all cities, and all countries, which have not a ready welcome to him who cometh

"In the name of the Lord,"

Who are more eager for their old customs, or for the preservation of their forms of etiquette, or for the trade that they have with some Edom or some Egypt, than they are to hear the Word of the Living God, and to welcome any messenger of His, though he be but a carpenter from the Hill-country, riding on an ass from the Highway.

"You drive me away," said Jesus sadly. "The time will come when you will need a message from God, and shall listen for it in vain.

Armies shall gird you in. These sacrifices shall be impotent to buy heaven's favor. These long prayers shall be flung back and their worthlessness be shown. In the fall of your pride, nay, in the ruin of your city, you may be willing to say what you chide these children for saying now,

" Blessed is he that cometh in the name of the Lord,".

Who comes in the name of the Eternal. He speaks the thing which is, and cannot change. I Am has sent him.

We should better catch the spirit of the scene, if the words, " the name of the Lord," thus expressed to us, what they expressed to them : the absolute Law, the Law of Eternity.

Here is one who comes in the name of the Eternal.

Imagine such an announcement brought of a sudden into a meeting of the real governors of one of our cities, Boston, Chicago, New York, or New Orleans. They have come together to agree about the appointments, to settle a quarrel in the Council Chamber, or to arrange about some votes with this or that leader of men. The door-keeper flings open the door and announces a stranger.

" Is he a delegate from any ward?"

" No."

" Has he a letter from Mr. Cleveland or Mr. Blaine?"

" Oh no."

" Does he represent the County Committee, or the State Committee?"

" Oh no."

" Then what is he here for? Send him away."

" Oh, he has come to tell us what is, what always is, and always must be. He comes in the name of the Eternal."

" Then we don't want him here. Let him hire a hall. Gentlemen, we will go on with our business."

It is exactly now, as it was then. We drop the idea from our Administration. We care only for the money that is dropped into the treasury, and for the outward forms of administration.

Compared with taxes, and loans, and buildings, and places,—this office and that office, this ring and that combination,—how slightly and feebly speaks the Eternal Word! How indifferent are men to this carpenter or that fisherman, who has no word to speak of adventure or of wealth, but has only the word of God to proclaim, and has no credentials but that he comes in the name of the Lord. This man comes to tell us of God's law of health, of what must be in our city if we would not have our children die. That man comes to tell us of God's law of purity, of what must be, if manhood is not to die out of our sons, and womanhood from our daughters. Another comes to tell us of the law of mutual service, that sons and daughters must bear each other's burdens. Another wants to tell us of mutual kindness and good-will, that nation must not lift up sword against nation, if the Kingdom is to come. Such a messenger never comes in state. There is never a trumpeter before nor a train of chariots and outriders. No, when they say, "Lo Here or Lo There," of such a messenger, you may be safe if you do not go after him nor follow him. His entry into your city is some humble ovation. Meek and lowly he comes to you, on the ass's colt he has picked up by the highway. It is not what he looks like which you are to judge by. It is the Word he has to speak to you. It is not the procession of his followers which gives him dignity. It is the name in which he comes. Blessed is he that cometh in the name of the Lord.

Wo indeed to Jerusalem, because she cannot see the infinite worth of such a prophet.

Blessing to any city which will look, not for the things that are seen, but at the Eternal truth which is not seen!

Blessing to any city, which will welcome any word which speaks and pleads for the eternal good even of the least of her little ones.

Blessing to any city, which is not so weighted down by the burdens of her own prosperity, but that she can look upward and forward to the true prosperity of the City of the Living God.

Blessing to any city, which to any voice of the Spirit of truth, has prompt and reverent answer; which from its heart, in its law, in its social order and in its daily life, will say,

"Blessed is he that cometh in the name of the Lord."

PALM SUNDAY.

BY JOHN KEBLE.

Ye whose hearts are beating high
With the pulse of Poesy,
Heirs of more than royal race,
Framed by Heaven's peculiar grace,
God's own work to do on earth,
   (If the word be not too bold,)
Giving virtue a new birth,
   And a life that ne'er grows old,—

Sovereign masters of all hearts!
Know ye who hath set your parts?
He who gave you breath to sing,
By whose strength ye sweep the string,
He has chosen you, to lead
   His Hosannas here below;—
Mount, and claim your glorious meed;
   Linger not with sin and woe.

But if ye should hold your peace,
Deem not that the song would cease.
Angels round His glory-throne,
Stars, His guiding hand that own,
Flowers that grow beneath our feet,
   Stones in earth's dark womb that rest,
High and low in choir shall meet,
   Ere His name shall be unblest.

Lord, by every minstrel tongue
Be Thy praise so duly sung,
That Thine angels' harps may ne'er
Fail to find fit echoing here:
We the while, of meaner birth,
  Who in that divinest spell
Dare not hope to join on earth,
  Give us grace to listen well.

But should thankless silence seal
Lips, that might half Heaven reveal,
Should bards in idol-hymns profane
The sacred, soul-enthralling strain,
(As in this bad world below
  Noblest things find vilest using,)
Then, Thy power and mercy show,
  In vile things noble breath infusing;

Then waken into sound divine
The very pavement of Thy shrine,
Till we, like Heaven's star-sprinkled floor,
Faintly give back what we adore.
Childlike though the voices be,
  And untunable the parts,
Thou wilt own the minstrelsy,
  If it flow from childlike hearts.

PASSION WEEK.

"Many believed on his name."—JOHN ii, 23.

THE record of the first public visit made to Jerusalem by the Saviour is that many believed on his name, but that Jesus did not trust himself unto them. Nicodemus, of whom only is any detail given, came to him by night to talk with him: and it seems as if this indicated his unwillingness to have the interview known. This was at the Passover in the early spring. Of his leaving that region this is the account, "When the Pharisees had heard that his disciples baptized more than John he left Judaea for Galilee." They were jealous of him and he went away.

The record of his second visit is that "the Jews persecuted Jesus," because he healed a man on the Sabbath day. " Then they sought the more to kill him because he spake of God as his own Father, making himself equal with God." That God was his Father and our Father, that we are all the children of God, was the first thing he had to teach and to make them feel. For this they sought to kill him.

When he came to Jerusalem the third time the people were saying, "When the Christ comes will he do more miracles than this man has done?" The Pharisees and chief priests on this sent officers to take him. But no one laid hands on him. The officers themselves came back to their chiefs and said, " Never man spake like this man." Day after day they stood face to face, the priests dreading him, and he earnestly pleading with them. Once they took up stones to cast at him, but he left the temple and passed away unhurt.

He was in Jerusalem again in the beginning of winter, at the Feast of the Dedication. It is just the same story again, with harder animosity on their part. They try to make him say he is the Messiah. He says he is the Son of God. They try to stone him, and he again escapes from their hands.

All these successive narratives enable us to stand in the place of these city Pharisees and Scribes, when for the fifth time this Nazarene comes down to Jerusalem, at the second Passover. His presence has been an annoyance at every visit: an annoyance which has developed into contest at the last. All the time the reputation of his movement on the East of Jordan, in Galilee, and even in the provinces beyond Galilee, is brought down to town. Who is he? What does he say he is? What does Herod think of him? Will Herod put him out of our way as he did John the Baptist? They say he has not been seen in Galilee for a few weeks past. Is there perhaps some hope that he will not come to this Feast at all?

They sought therefore for Jesus and said among themselves, as they stood in the temple, "What think ye, that he will not come to the Feast? Now both the chief priests and Pharisees had given commandment that if any man knew where he was, he should declare it that they might take him." Their policy has been completely indicated by Caiaphas. The Council said, "If we suffer this man to go on thus, all will believe on him: and the Romans will come and take away our place and our nation." To whom Caiaphas replied, "Ye know nothing nor do ye consider that it is expedient for us that one man should die for the people."

They are but the most broken fragments of a history, all these little hints which lead us along from step to step of their increasing hatred. But the longest annals, in the nicest detail, would hardly make a more distinct picture. If any one had told Nicodemus or his companions at the first Passover, that they would kill the Galilean, brutally, and with the whole force of the mob of Jerusalem, they would have cried, "Never." He was of no such consequence. Indeed he seems, in some regards, "a very amiable and deserving young man," they would have said, if only he were not upset by his notion that he came direct from God. But month by month goes by, summer, autumn, winter, he never changes; and they, alas! do change. The spring season comes on. The preparations for the Festival go forward. There is, as I said, just the hope that he will not come at all, and that all ceremony may go forward in the good old way, when, on the day after the Sabbath, in the midst of the pilgrims from the East and North, here is a throng, a procession, cheering, and singing, "Hosanna to the Son of David!" "Blessed is he that cometh in the name of the Lord!" "Hosanna in the Highest!" Palm leaves are scattered in the streets. Children are shouting and singing in the temple. And here—as calmly as if we had never driven him out last year—here comes again the Nazarene carpenter.

"Who is this?"

"This is Jesus, the prophet from Nazareth of Galilee."

And he has abated no jot from last year's pretensions. Just as he did before he drives the hucksters from the temple courts. "My Father's house a house of merchandise!" And when they come to him to ask him to do, what they cannot do, and silence these boys cheering with enthusiasm:

"I tell you, if these should hold their peace, the stones would immediately cry out!"

He has not receded. Not he. He comes in triumph now, where last year he came secretly and alone. Unless priest and Pharisee take a stand, who shall say what will come? The whole tragedy culminates therefore. Every hour shows how it culminates. "The chief Priests and the Scribes and the Leaders of the people sought how they might destroy him: and they could not find what they might do, for all the people were eagerly attentive to hear him." And the next morning: "Tell us by what authority doest thou these things, and who gave thee this authority?" I will also ask you one thing. "The baptism of John, was it from heaven or of men?" That is a hard question. If they say, "From heaven." "Why did *ye* not receive him?" But if we say, "From men." Ah, "We are afraid of the people. For all the people held John as a prophet." So they had to say, "We do not know." "Then I do not tell you by what authority I do these things. But what think ye? A certain man had two sons, and he came to the first and said, Son, go, work to-day in my vineyard." And with this beginning he goes on, just as he did when he first preached at Nazareth, to compare outcast with Pharisee; child of sin, with child of Abraham; to show that God had no Peculiar People; that if the Gentiles did His will He was as well pleased as if the Jews did it. "Verily I say unto you, the publicans and the harlots go into the Kingdom of God before you. For John came unto you in the way of righteousness, and ye believed him not. But the publicans believed him. Yes, the very harlots believed him,—and ye, although ye saw that, changed not your thought that ye might believe him. And I will tell you another parable. There was a householder who planted a vineyard—"

And from that beginning he went on to paint the picture of Israel's steady decline and fall. We are used to it. We have read it and heard it read, with spirit or without, mechanically or eagerly. But, after all the mechanism or rote of eighteen centuries, it is still a terrible picture, as you see at last the crisis. "What will the lord of the vineyard do? He will come and destroy these husbandmen, he will give the fruit to others!" Everybody was moved. Everybody was excited with the prophecy. "God forbid, God forbid!" they groaned. And he looked on them and said, "Have ye not read this scripture, 'The stone that the builders rejected, has become the head stone of the cornice?' The Kingdom of God will be taken from you and be given to a nation bringing forth the fruits thereof."

"They knew he spake of them," says the simple record. Of course they knew it. But they feared the people. Of course they feared the people. It is worth remembering, that though the people is figured only by that low mob of Jerusalem, the People is already born. They left him and went away.

He did not go away. He began again. "The Kingdom of Heaven is like a man who made a marriage-feast." And with this story, just as he did at the beginning at Nazareth, he shows how the guests invited reject the feast, and those from the highways and the by-ways enjoy it. It is the only thing he will say to them: that the sons of Abraham have no precedence, have flung away all advantage; feast, kingdom, life, heaven, are the equal blessing of every child of God. There are none base born! All are of the blood royal!

Then they try to catch him in sedition, or to break him down before the people. "Shall we give tribute to Cæsar?" "What is the great commandment?" "Which brother of these seven should marry this woman in the other world you talk of?" But he turns the tables here, and from that moment there is no more questioning. No! They are too angry—and he is too sad. He speaks his last word of protest. "Woe unto you, Scribes and Pharisees." He will not die without showing such hypocrisy for what it is. "On you will come all the righteous blood shed upon the earth! Yes, it will come on this very generation!"

"Oh Jerusalem, Jerusalem, which killest the prophets, and stonest these who have been sent unto thee! How often would I have gathered thy children together as a hen gathereth her chickens under her wings, and ye would not! Behold, your house is left to you desolate. Ye will not see me henceforth until ye shall say,

"Blessed is he that cometh in the name of the Lord."

And he went out and departed from the temple, and never entered it again.

"Ye shall seek me and ye shall not find me, and whither I go ye cannot come." This had been a part of his farewell.

"Will he go to the dispersed among the Gentiles?" Not he. That is a question which such men put, and they only. He knows that this is the hour, or "that his time has come." And he awaits the issue with his friends. For these friends he speaks the last words of instruction or of warning. With these friends he joins in the New Year's festival of their nation; sitting as a father would sit at a Thanksgiving feast, he asks them all to remember him, and to remember him always. And they go over to the Mount of Olives as is their custom, and he parts from them to go into the garden at the foot of the hill to pray.

I am not trying to follow his life nor theirs. I am trying to trace this history as it unrolled for these dignitaries of the temple; these priests and senators who were leading Jerusalem and Israel to their ruin. These men, by the natural downward haste of bigotry, these men, who, last year, would have laughed you to scorn, if you told them that a carpenter from Nazareth could turn them from their track, this way or hat way, these men have in successive months gone through all the stages of hatred. They have warned people not to harbor him. They have warned them not to come near him. They have tried to arrest him, they have tried to stone him and have failed. And now, they have tried to make him commit himself in the presence of their rulers and of his, and they have failed again. The people cannot be relied upon. The people are not sorry to listen to parable or invective so bravely spoken against the petty oligarchy which struts its hour and keeps them under. The people may be on this side, may be on that side. But we, chief priests and senators, we are nowhere unless this Nazarene is put down before this week is over. Why, there has not been a feast since he came to the surface, in which he has not been the chief and we ridiculed as if captives in his royal train!

It is to such men that there comes, just after one of these invectives, Judas Iscariot, the thirteenth in the Nazarene's company, who has given to that number, thirteen, a bad name, from that day to this day. He has blighted his own name with the same blight, so that the proud name of Judah, Lion among the tribes of Israel, prince and king, has not since he died been given to any child in the Christendom he did not crush, no, though Judah were also the name of a brother of the Lord. And Iscariot, the name that night of a village on the slope of Edom, is since that night the definition of traitor in every language spoken in Christian lands. To these puzzled, hateful, angry lords of an expiring oligarchy, distrustful of themselves, of their own officers, of their own future, there comes their fit coadjutor and companion, Judas Iscariot the traitor. "I will betray him to you." "For how much?" "Well! would you give as much as 30 pieces of silver?" "It is a bargain." And on that great bargain they clasp hands.

So that while Jesus and his own are still at supper, while he is saying in the last prayer, "Those that thou gavest me I have kept, and none of them is lost, but perdition's child," Judas is in the presence of the rulers, they are telling off the guards, men are looking at the blades of their swords, are swinging their clubs, are falling into order in the shade of the guard-house, that the bright moon may not show that any arrest is planned. He counts his hours rightly. He leads them also across Kedron. He enters beneath the olive trees into the court of the garden, where Jesus is just awakening the three sleepers for the last time. No question whom to arrest, for the traitor pushes his way into the group, "'Hail, Master,' and kissed him."

"Who is it that you seek?" he says to them.

"Jesus of Nazareth."

"I am he. If you seek me, take me, and let these go." So careful, from the first, of his friends.

"Are you come out against me as if I were a midnight robber, with your clubs and your swords? I have been sitting daily with you in the temple, and you laid no hands on me. But this is your hour, and the power of darkness." Meanwhile they are binding him, and they lead him away.

In these preludes you have the key-note for all the examinations, all the taunts, all the doubts of that tedious night, and for all the cruelty of the next day. By the time the sun is risen and the people of the city are abroad, the plot is far enough forward for any fear of the people to be dismissed. A mob is very terrible, but it is very fickle and it sides very fatally with the stronger party. "Let our criminal be stripped and bound, let him be kept where he cannot speak to this cursed people; give us a chance to contrast Barabbas, their favorite, against this Nazarene whom they hardly know, and we can manage the people. Nay, we can turn the people against this Pilate, he is cursed, too." On the weakness of Pilate hung the fortunes of that day.

They play off Pilate against the mob, and the mob against Pilate. Hour after hour the tumult quickens. The narrow streets of the little city see this procession and that procession, as the King of the Jews is sent to Herod, and as Herod sends him back to the Romans. All Pilate's force is under arms, never doubt that. But what a handful, when you think of this Asiatic mob, hating him, hating them, and hating the Cæsar for whom he stands and they. The end can be foretold from the beginning. "When Pilate saw therefore that he could prevail nothing," but that an insurrection was before him, what was one peasant's life, more or less, to Pilate, or to Rome? "He took water and washed his hands before them."

"I am innocent of the blood of this just person."

"Then delivered he him unto them to be crucified."

That is an awful picture, which a great master has drawn, of the horror of the conspirators, after their plot has succeeded, after he is nailed to the cross and hangs there dying. What would not every man of them do, even Annas, even Caiaphas, if he could undo the horrid work of that fatal day? Notice how each actor whom we see in it begs us to know that it is no deed of his.

Poor Pilate disappears from the story, saying, "I am innocent of the blood of this just man."

The centurion who obeyed because Rome bade him, as he would have stood at his post had Mt. Zion vomited fire, said while he obeyed, "Truly this was a righteous man."

The women of Jerusalem wept as he passed by.

And though one of these poor thieves charged him with being the cause of their death, the other bravely says, "He has done nothing amiss." Nay, Annas and Caiaphas themselves, only a few weeks after, shake off the charge with a ghastly indignation, when they ask the apostles if they mean to bring this man's blood upon them. And when poor Judas stammers out, "I have sinned in that I have betrayed innocent blood," they stammer in reply, "What is that to us? What is that to us? See thou to that." If the night of Friday closes in with abject wretchedness to John, and James, and Andrew, and Peter, what is it to Annas, and Caiaphas, and Alexander, and the rest of them?

There are two who have not consented nor borne part in their act, "faithful among the faithless," two out of seventy rulers of Israel, whose eye is clear enough to look beyond Israel, and they bear the body and lay it tenderly in the new tomb, in the garden hard by the place where he was crucified. They roll a great stone to the entrance of the tomb, and in the night again, after such a day, leave it there with the reverence due to death. And Mary Magdalene was there, with the other Mary, sitting over against the sepulchre.

And do you remember that their service of this very morning is a service of death? It is because he is dead, because they know that he is dead, that they bear their spices for his embalmment! What is to them that mystic prophecy of his of the third day? They have seen him die and they know the end too well.

What is it to Peter and Andrew, to James and John, to Philip and Nathaniel and the rest? Had they not hoped for, almost seen, the Kingdom? And now where is the King? Have they not been preaching, "The Kingdom of God is here"? And now what mockery in every word of that proclamation, and in every triumphant welcome which it received. So is it that that Sabbath, last of Jewish Sabbaths, is the longest, darkest, blackest day of history.

For the next morning, on this day, "the first day of the week," says the writer,—why does he not say the first day of the new record of the world?—" very early in the morning," even as the first gray light of the sun dawns, these women are there with their spices—and the tomb is empty.

> " O grave, where is thy victory?
> O death, where is thy sting?"

The Past is past forever! The old world of death and tears and terror is really done with. The world of Pilate, and Barabbas, and Judas, and Caiaphas, and such as they, has won its last real triumphs.

The new world, the world of life, and joy, and hope, the world of saints and of martyrs, the world of sons of consolation and princes of peace, has this day begun.

There will be pretended victories, as when Nero beheads Paul and crucifies Peter, as when Julian tries to set back the hand upon the dial, as when Rome again, as by the hand of another Pilate, burns Huss at the stake. But never a real victory!

There will be things men call failure, as when Wycliffe's ashes are scattered to the seas, or when Coligny falls dead in the massacre of St. Bartholomew, but never a final failure of the right.

John, James, Peter, Andrew, Mary, Salome, the Magdalene, see now what the real kingdom is, and how it is to be won. So on this resurrection morning is born the infant church, ready for its victories. And the cry of joy of Mary Magdalene welcomes it to the world which it is to save.

THIRST.

BY FREDERIKA BREMER.

"I THIRST! — O, grant the waters pure,
Which flowed by Eden's rosy bower;
The glorious, fresh, and silver stream,
The ever young, whose flashing gleam
Once before angel footsteps rolled;
Whose sands were wisdom's priceless gold.

"I thirst! — O bounteous source of Truth,
Give coolness to my fevered youth;
Make the sick heart more strong and wise;
Take spectral visions from mine eyes;
O, let me quench my thirst in thee,
And pure, and strong, and holy be!

"I thirst! — O God, great Source of Love!
Infinite Life streams from above.
O, give one drop, and let me live!
The barren world has nought to give;
No solace have its streams for me;
I thirst alone for heaven and thee."

THE VICTORY.

"Lift up your heads, O ye gates; and be lifted up, ye everlasting doors, and the King of Glory shall come in."—PSALMS, xxiv, 9.

IN the fancies of the early church the supposed descent of Christ into Hell in the period between his crucifixion and his resurrection, was a favorite subject of discourse and song. Such discourse and song have left their track all through the literature and even the theology of Christendom. You will find in Dante this and that reference to Christ's bearing in Hell made as distinctly as any reference to his life as recorded in the Gospel. All this structure of phantasy is founded on the words in the Epistle ascribed to Peter, which say he preached to the spirits in prison, and on the corresponding words in the Apostles' Creed which say he descended into Hell.

Of these words in the Creed, I suppose the whole meaning to have been that his death was real. But they were sufficient foundation for the poets of the early church to build upon, and they built gorgeous fabric of infernal legend. We are to remember that in days when to attack the reigning powers of earth would have wrought misery to their cause, they might say with impunity what they chose, as to the ruling powers of Hell.

In such legend the words of the twenty-fourth Psalm, which we have sung to-day, "Lift up your heads, oh, ye gates!" were applied to the gates of Hell, those gates over which Dante writes the words, "All hope abandon, ye who enter here."

The heavy iron portal spiked above and bolted beneath, is, at the word, to slide upward in its grooves, and leave the pathway beneath it open for the King. "Lift up your heads; rise up before him." In imagery like that to which Paradise Lost has accustomed us, the Prince of Tartarus is represented as taunting Satan for his failures in attempting to overthrow Jesus and his Kingdom. "Of a sudden," says Epiphanius in a sermon on this subject, "a voice of thunder was heard in which Gabriel and Michael and an escort of angels gave to the astonished host of Hell this old and eternal order: 'Princes, lift up your gates! Be lifted up, ye everlasting doors! and the King of Glory shall come in.'

"The Prince of Tartarus raged anew when he heard this sound, turned against Satan and said to him, 'Go, fight this King of Glory.' Then to his own servants: 'Close the gates of brass; push home the bolts of iron, and resist him to the last, lest we ourselves be taken captive.' But the imprisoned saints, who, under hellish power, have been kept there awaiting their Redeemer, cried out to the Prince of Hell, 'Open your gates that the King of Glory may come in.' and as they made this cry the voice of the chorus of angels from the outside was heard again, 'Princes of Hell, lift up your gates! Be lifted up, ye everlasting doors, and the King of Glory shall come in!'

"Frightened and trembling, the Prince of Hell asks, 'Who is the King of Glory?' and it is given to David, one of his prisoners now, to take up the words which he had sung a thousand years before, when the rude portcullis of Jerusalem first shot up to give an entrance to the rescued Ark. 'The Lord, strong and mighty. The Lord mighty in battle. He is the King of Glory,' and at these words brass, iron, and adamant crumble and disappear.

"The Lord Jesus in his human form enters and enlightens Hell. He breaks all bonds. He releases all captives by his infinite power."

We are not to suppose that poet or preacher who repeated these legends to the church of the fourth or fifth century, had any more definite belief that these were literal facts than had the poet Milton, that the events which he describes, either in Hell or in Paradise, were visible and actual occurrences. There was many a reason in those ages why poet or preacher should prefer to describe the Christian triumph in a parable, than by naming in separate detail the princes who were to be overthrown or the shrines which were to be destroyed. It is only in the decline of spiritual faith and in the consequent hardening blindness of that idolatry which always makes the image of more worth than the idea, that such fancies made their way into the mythology of the Middle Ages, and in the end took their part in that mass of clumsy legend, which from the eyes of an eager world shut out the vision of a loving God. The legend itself, for any one who will recall it, in the simplicity in which it originally formed itself, is the enthusiastic triumph of a world new born, for its deliverance from sin, from death and the grave, from whatever princes of Hell and whatever kings of wickedness! It is simply the song of triumph which declared that for the future there is no grave and is no Hell, such as old terrors had imagined. It proclaims that there are no powers of earth which can stand for an instant against the simple power of Heaven. It proclaims that there is no death when God's children, resting in His arms and quickened by His love, have once learned what life is, and what its infinite sway. The legend, in its fashion, if you please in its clumsy fashion, strikes the key-note thus early, of all Christian literature and of all Christian song. For you may take this as a general and central principle in criticism, that all science, literature or song, which recognizes conscious life as the ruling principle of the universe, is Christian. On the other hand, all science, literature and song, which makes you believe in things or afraid of things or think that things can be, unmastered by the powers of life, is such science, literature, or song, as in such legends were rightly characterized as belonging to Hell and to the Devil.

It sometimes seems easier to trace the great general laws of God's government in the passage of events far from us, than in those close around us. We see the shape of those far-off constellations, but we cannot group or set in order that to which our own sun belongs. It is easier then, perhaps, to see how life conquered death, how spirit conquered form, how the idea dethroned the image in those days of the new-born church, than in these whose dust and smoke are around us. Of the victories of Life then, these preachers and poets hardly dared speak, except in such allegories as I have read to you. Till the day Christ died, Force, Brute Force ruled the world, that was the principle of the great Roman Empire. It was the organization of human power. At the head of that organization Tiberius sat upon his lonely throne. One of the arms of that organization lay across conquered Judah. And when the moment came, the tool of that organization, Pontius Pilate, nailed Jesus Christ to the cross. Did he die? Can a kingdom like his kingdom die? The Idea with which he had inoculated the world cannot die. It *is* Life—that is its name. This Idea when he died, seemed to live only in the faith and hope and love of a few weeping women and as many ignorant men. Yes. But it did live there. And, because it lived there, it has met, in a thousand battle-fields; nay, on a thousand crosses, with the Brute Force which till now has mastered the world. It is like the old battle of Hercules with the Hydra. The child of Eternal Life meets the hundred-headed dragon of the Deeps. And it seems as if, for every dragon head that is lopped off, two more terrible appear. Seems so. But in truth Life is gaining all the while. Brute force, such power as there seems to be in things, cannot stand against ideas which are eternal. And the groans of the King of Tartarus, and of Satan, Prince of Evil, only represent under a metaphor the successive ruins of every bloody superstition, of every form of slavery, of every cruelty, of patrician scorn, of every lust of every Claudius and Caligula, which one after another give way, as the Lord of Life, whom they crucified, begins his reign. Pilate nailed Jesus Christ to the cross. Yes! And which was the stronger ten years after, Pilate, or this crucified Saviour? The Roman Emperor was master, and the Nazarene was crucified like a felon. Yes; and which was the stronger, when one or two centuries had rolled by, the Emperor of Rome still representing the brute force of the world, organized never so deftly and wisely, or the crucified Nazarene? Or, if from that day to this day we come down, what shall we say of all the thrones and dominions and principalities and powers, which have nothing but physical force to rely upon? Thrones, dominations, principalities, know now with a terrible certainty that mere force of arms has no power which compares with that living word of the crucified Nazarene, that bears with it Eternal Life, and directs the duty of a world of men whom he can lead, but who bend no knee to power.

Yet this lesson of Easter, the victory of Life over method, force, and form needs to be asserted and maintained, as much in our time as ever. We are always falling back into the conceited notion that we can devise some machinery, which will do instead of hearty, resolute Life, of brave and godly living. As in the beginning, they ate of the tree of knowledge instead of the tree of Life. For instance, there grows up in our crowded civilization, a blighted growth of pauperism, crime, drunkenness, parent and child of pauperism and crime, lust and beggary. There is enough godly life in the world, for men to look with horror on such hell in the midst of them. And, as they ought, they devise this poor law, that tax, such and such restrictions, such and such prisons, and then really expect that because their machinery is so ingenious, and the science of the thing so nicely adjusted, the whole evil will cease, that the paupers will be rich, and the licentious pure, and the thieves honest, and the sick well. Fools and blind! All this is like the invention of perpetual motion. The water rises in your new hydraulic combination, yes, it rises to just the height where you poured it in, there and no higher. The lever moves in your exquisitely ordered machinery. Yes, it moves just so far as you push it, so far and no farther. To open these blind eyes, to feed this starving crew, to heal these scrofulous beggars, to give back these wasted infants to Rachel who is weeping for her children, and will not be comforted, you need Life; you need the living, loving heart of living, loving men and women to quicken other hearts which can live too and love too, and in their turn will quicken others which are dying now. The better your machinery, the simpler and the easier your work. But you fall back into heathenism, and into these lurid fights of Satan against Pluto, if you suppose that any machinery of your law, your taxes or your social science, is going to do what only life can do. It is when Life and Love come forward in their triumph, that these gates of hell crumble and are gone. Lift up your heads, O ye gates, and be ye lifted up, ye everlasting doors, that the King of Glory may come in!

We fall into the same mistake if we train our children to the knowledge of things and methods, and let the divine life in them dwindle and die away, the life which ought to manage methods and handle things. How miserable a pretender the wordy orator, who has such store of language, such grace of gesture, a presence so attractive, but has, alas, nothing to say! Or this writer, who sends to the hard-pressed editor her reams of paper covered with lines of the right length and rhymes of the right jingle, the large letters in their places and the small ones in theirs, but all cold and dead, because there is no spark of faith, or hope, or love. As for accomplishment, whether of body or of mind, it has always had one law. Unless it were under the control, absolute and unflinching, of this Living Soul,—God-given regent of mind and body,—all accomplishment has been Satan and Mephistopheles, tempter to evil and ruin. In the court of Tiberius, in the palace of Nero, there were accomplished women and learned men. They did not play the piano, but they played on something as hard to learn as the piano. They did not calculate percentages, or arrange to make corners in the food market. But they did use brains that were quite as fine as ours in computations that were quite as difficult. And none of this accomplishment, nicety, or finesse saved them or helped them to be saved. There was no life in these palaces or courts. The Life had died out of them, till one day, a prisoner who had pleaded before Nero spoke a word and another word which some servant of the household heard: the word of Life, which is Power, and the only Power, and in that word they began to live. Our finest accomplishment and our most recondite learning are as worthless as theirs, till they spring into life at the touch of the same magic wand, and unless they maintain life by the same talisman.

I have spent a few days past in a region where the historical memorials, and indeed some of the customs of to-day, carry us back to that time which begins to seem mythical, when the Mayflower ran into the bay at Provincetown, and found rest from long heaving and tossing. In her cabin, as she lay there, was signed the first compact of government. From her anchorage men went forth on the explorations which were the beginning of an Empire. We linger fondly, we cannot linger too fondly, on the records of their faith, and hope, and love. But is there man, woman, or child of us who would go back to that life, to live it as they lived it? I say nothing of physical hardship. I do not ask whether we should like starvation, and cold, and loneliness like theirs, though I might ask that fairly. Would any man or woman of us, who have seen the vision of to-day, and know what to-day is achieving, go back to the narrowness of their interests, to the pettiness of their thought, to the range so circumscribed of their occupations and meditations? Not one of us who has imagination enough to conceive what that half life was, or who can to-day put any fair estimate on the possibility of to-day! And this is simply to say that all those visions of old prophecy are working their accomplishment in every home. He who sits upon the white horse goes forth conquering and to conquer. Not in the fashion which John of Patmos thought of, very likely. But in God's fashions, a thousand times more grand, for victories a thousand times more sure. He overthrows death, he conquers ignorance and sin, crime is more hated, truth is more honored. Light overpowers darkness, good conquers evil. And if this is true here, it is only because it is true everywhere. Those Pilgrim Fathers were not little men, nor mean, nor bad. They did the largest thing done in their time, and it showed faith most vividly. But everywhere, as time passes, the eternal law is, that the power which works for Righteousness succeeds, which is to say that God reigns, or that His Kingdom comes.

It is ours to enter into the victory. It is ours to refuse the cares of smoke and dust, of the things that perish, and to enter into the reality of Infinite Life. Ours to live as those

"Who live and move and have their being in their God."

Of this daily miracle of what *is* over what seems, the miracle of Easter is the great commemoration. Indeed, the word miracle does not mean any magic trick, setting aside the order of nature, it means the assertion of the spirit over the forms and methods of dead matter. When the Master of Life commands the life of one who trusts him to move the paralyzed arm, the living soul obeys and the dead limb does his will. On the morning of this great miracle the living soul returned to the body it had left, for the strength, the comfort, the new life of these weeping women and these doubting men. In that return to earth, though it were only to say farewell again, in those few days, though they had no new lesson to teach, the Lord of Life quickened their lives that they might truly live. From that open tomb they went forth on the mission of New Life to which he sent them. The world of dead force was to be a world ruled by hope and faith. The world of fear was to be a world of love. The world of tyrant and slave was to be a world of brother and brother. The world of death was to be a world of life. Northward, southward, eastward, westward, they went forth to this mission of life. Living, dying, teaching, blessing, comforting and curing, they were true to this mission. And the symbol of Easter morning fulfills itself every hour, as the tears of the world are wiped away, and its sorrows healed. It was dead and is alive again. It was lost and is found.

" Lift higher your gates, ye princes of the people, and be ye lifted up, ye everlasting doors, and the King of Glory shall come in."

SOLACE IN SORROW.

BY AUBREY DE VERE.

Count each affliction, whether light or grave,
God's messenger sent down to thee. Do thou
With courtesy receive him; rise and bow,
And ere his shadow pass thy threshold, crave
Permission first his heavenly feet to lave.
Then lay before him all thou hast, allow
No cloud of passion to usurp thy brow
Or mar thy hospitality, no wave
Of mortal tumult to obliterate
The soul's marmoreal calmness. Grief should be
Like joy; majestic, equable, sedate,
Confirming, cleansing, raising, making free;
Strong to consume small troubles, to commend
Great thoughts, grave thoughts, thoughts lasting
    to the end.

LIFE AND ITS ENEMIES.

"God hath given unto us Eternal Life, and this Life is in his Son."— I. JOHN v, ii.

ASK any simple Christian to tell you, in brief, the story of Christ's Life; ask a child, or a savage who cannot read. He will say: "The Jews hated him. Pilate tried to kill him. But he still lives, and will live forever." This is a sufficient abridgment of the gospel.

Such an abridgment has its value, because when you thus come down to the Rock,—as Jesus himself would say,—when you state the real foundation of the Christian religion,—you find it is Life. The shrewdness of the shifty Jew and the force of the organizing and brutal Roman take their fit rank of subordination. The Christian religion asserts itself again in Christ's own words, the motto of this Church:—

"I am come that they might have *Life*, and might have it more abundantly."

Easter Sunday becomes the Sunday of Sundays, because it renews this statement, that Life is the one essential. In the face of ritual, of any formality or other physical corruption of religion, it asserts that Life is the essential. And, in the face of dogma, enforced creed,—logical plan of salvation wrought out by intellectual process,—it asserts that Life is the essential. It may serve us, if we review the gospel stories and find how this statement is the centre of what they say.

Jesus is so determined to enliven men that it seems, at the beginning, as if he could not believe that they would cling to their grave-clothes so desperately. His encounters with rabbinical learning and with decorous establishments, of which the whole effort was to conform to what is written,—encounters all full of his protest against what is superficial or merely transitory,—are, in fact, like the dash of the eternal sea upon the rock. The looker-on thinks the sea is repulsed, and that it is the cliff which triumphs. It is only after a century that you see that the cliff has been ground away, and that the eternal sea is still beating upon other ledges which time has disclosed. There is no better illustration of the absurdities of literalism—of the follies of holding by a code which is antiquated, of the vanity of knowledge as distinguished from wisdom—than this illustration, given by the conflict between the living Jesus—life-giving—and these mummies, the literalist rabbin, the law-abiding Pharisees of his time.

But he has to meet, not the learning of the time only, but the brute force of the time as well,—a carpenter's son on one side, and the Emperor Tiberius and the power of the Roman Empire on the other. John's disciples, crazy with indignation, come storming around him in Galilee to make him King of the Jews. That is enough to compromise him. The garrison at Tiberias sends down word to the other garrisons that there is another rising and another king. Pilate has heard of him before the gray of that morning, when the chief priests bring him before his judgment. The wit and craft of Asia unite with the force of arms of Europe to trample out this spark of the Light Divine. "Did he say 'more life'? We nail him to the cross." That is what Learning says, that is what the Right Arm of Power says when you talk of "Life—more abundantly."

And after the Learning of Asia and the Force of Europe have done their worst, here are these women, testifying that the grave cannot hold him. "And, before we know it, here are these followers of his, preaching in the temple courts, just as he did—pestilent fellow!—at the Passover. Is there no end to this thing? Will it never die?"

No. That is just what it will not do. It will not die. It is all through Jerusalem. They have caught the flavor of it at Damascus. "Why, these Samaritans—cursed heathen!—have heard of it at Neapolis. Down in Africa, that treasurer has carried it, whom we had here with the offerings from Æthiopia; and in Antioch, they say, half the synagogues are mad with it. Do you remember that Saul—quick-witted, eager fellow—at Gamaliel's school? He has gone into this new way. He is all over Greece proclaiming it." Such are the ejaculations of the next twenty years. Clearly enough, this thing does not die easily.

"Were they right, who said we did not kill him on Calvary?" Yet the history of "the New Way," as they called it, is always on the same lines as the history of him who led the way. Always the wit of man is trying to out-manœuvre it, or the force of man trying to crush out its Life. There was never an enemy to the Life more dangerous than that wordy Learning of those first centuries. All their cumbrous Egyptian triad-system, three gods who are one God, has to be grafted into it. No religion can meet the fashion of Alexandria, can meet the popular taste, which has not its trinity. So the poor Christian Church, which started as absolute religion, has to take on that bit of philosophical costume. Then comes in the Persian system of two gods, a good god and a bad god; and the philosophers and creed-makers have to adapt the poor simple faith to these demands. "Freedom of will and foreordination, what do you say to them?" This is the cry of Augustine and the metaphysicians. And so another set of chains have to be riveted there. Poor, simple "Way of God," which began with "love God, love man, and live for heaven,"—one does not wonder if its victories stopped, when it was handicapped in the race by such dead weights as these. All this is to make the wisdom of men take the place of the abundant Life, which is, indeed, the very Life of God. Nor has "the Life made manifest" any harder experience through the ages than in the midst of those hopeless controversies. While men are pushing their words hither and thither, from this square to that, trying to make this statement fit with that, and that with another—changing the order to meet this or that inconsistency, and, after all, finding that the fatal block will not come true in the arrangement,—"The Life" is no longer manifested. In that puzzle, a new paralysis steals over the race which had begun to live.

And, at the same time, the "Christian Way" was repeating the Master's sorrows on the other side. The Master had to meet the craft of Caiaphas and his Pharisees. He had to meet as well the force of Pilate and his legions. The Life is always suffering between bodily passion and mental subtlety. While the Church had its very life-blood sucked out of it by those vampires of dogmatics, it was, without knowing it, dying out in the embrace of that very Roman Empire whose anger it met in the beginning. In the long run, the friendship of the Emperor Constantine has proved a heavier weight to it than the hatred of Nero and Diocletian. You cannot think of a worse gift for this "Way of Life," or for its loyal professors, than to receive it at court, to clothe them in the silk and purple and fine linen of Constantinople, to feed them with its luxuries, and to give to them its patronage. Look in those centuries for the "Life made manifest," and you have to search for a jewel in a dung-heap. And one can well imagine the Enemy of Souls of their mythology chuckling with Satanic glee when he sees "the Life," which Pilate could not crucify and Caiaphas could not extinguish, stifled at the court of Constantine or Justinian, under the mitres, the flounces, and the embroidery of an archbishop's uniform.

Dead, embalmed, and buried indeed is your Manifested Life in the history of some centuries,—with all the show of an Egyptian mummy or a cathedral tomb, and with as little life; with etiquette and ritual, with gorgeous pomp and lines of hierarchical service which only the court of the lower empire could have taught, and with as much heart and soul as that court knew—and as little.

From such death and burial the resurrection comes in some valley of the Alps, where the mountaineers read the simple gospel of Him who is the Way, the Truth, and the Life. They reject all priests and bishops and kings. They accept no sacraments nor other ordinances than they find his instruction for.

The resurrection comes when Peter Waldo, in Lyons,—under the shadow of a gray cathedral, in the government of a political archbishop, and a circle of political priests,—creates the people's Bible, copies the Gospels, the "Noble Lesson," as he calls it, for men to read in their own tongue.

It comes in Toulouse, and in all that lovely Southern France,—where, with new refinement in life, with a new beginning of civilization, religion also assumes a gentler and simpler form, rejects of course the politics of Rome and the materialism of her ritual,—to be crushed out, of course, in blood and fire and death, by the cruelty of Dominic and of Pope "Innocent."

The resurrection comes one day when Martin Luther, climbing on his knees the steps of the Roman stairway, where tradition tells him that such climbing shall buy off some years from purgatory, sees the lie and denounces it. He sees that Life knows nothing of such formalism.

"Thou shalt be justified *by faith*," by the inward certainty of the help of God.

The Christian Life rose from the dead in that uprising of the nations which we call The Reformation. And then, too, in the centuries which follow, the same history repeats itself again. The Enemy of Souls, you might say, moves out his heavy castle on the board, on the one side, and the shifty bishop, on the other, against this poor little pawn, who is not yet queen of the world. For a generation, in the enthusiasm of new life, the men and women of Christ's way did open blind eyes and deaf ears: they made the lame to walk, and what had been dead to live. They subdued kingdoms, wrought righteousness, obtained promises, stopped the mouths of lions, quenched the violence of fire, waxed valiant in fight, and seemed to promise a new kingdom. No Enemy of Souls could have routed such an army of those who had found out what the Law of Life was, if he had met them in square battle. But, when they begin to teach each other how it is, and why, then the temptation comes. "What was God doing before he made the world?" "What did God foreordain, and what came of his foreordination?" "How does God's justice in this business fit in with his mercy?" You know that string of dreary questions and their hopeless answers. The older among you remember the traces of them in your catechisms. You know how the new Life ebbs away and dies when all this splitting of hairs and instructing the Almighty come in. The power and miracle of the Life had been promised to babes, and not to the prudent or the wise. The power had come, and the miracles had been wrought, by those whom the world called foolish,—by those who were humble. And the moment when it seemed necessary to call on the universities of Europe to explain Christianity, or those learned in language or in logic to teach it,—in that moment it proved that the eagle had lost the balance of his wings, and could not fly; the virgin had lost her chastity: the lion had lost his teeth and his claws: the Life was buried again beneath the weight of logic and learning.

And the other lesson repeats itself as well. Your new Life in the freshness of its new birth, in the loveliness of this new simplicity,—

"When unadorned, adorned the most,"—

is tempted, just as she was tempted before, into the alliance of princes and potentates. It is just the old story over again. It is the old, false victory of the lying romances,—because she is simple. Your lovely maiden from the hillside, who is lovely precisely because she does not know the follies of courts, their etiquettes and frauds,—is seen by the king as he is hunting with his train. And he falls in love with her. Of course he falls in love with her. He has never seen such loveliness at court as that loveliness. Nay, he never knew such power as that simple power. Nay, he never heard such wisdom as falls from those lips untaught. And so he marries her and takes her to his palace. And there the romance always ends, in the chiming of bells, in the blaze of bonfires, and in the brilliancy of illumination. Yes, there the romance has to end. For from that moment the poor girl's loveliness declines, and her power ebbs, and her simple wisdom stammers. She is lost in these intrigues of courts, and in the damned falsity of their etiquettes. She cannot lift them by her own arm, and what happens is that they pull her down to their level. This is just what happens to your Christian Church,—to your simple New Life just born again, so lovely, so free, so pure, and so sweet,—when the kings of the earth come and make their court to her. Harry VIII. in England, Henry IV. in France, the Elector Frederick, or King Gustavus Adolphus, are only so many passionate and selfish princes, just for a moment bewitched by the eternal charm of purity and freedom, but no more able than Nicodemus was, to be born again into like purity and like freedom. You know what comes of such alliances, you know what must come of them. Farewell to your hope there of the coming kingdom! No more hosannas for the Prince of Peace! Farewell to your pæans of triumph in the liberty with which Christ makes you free! Farewell to your glad hymns, to the spirit of Life in Christ Jesus! This is not life which stammers out its prayers in words which a king directs. No: there is no such death as in the slavery of an exacted form.

Whoever toils, blind with dust and well-nigh hopeless, in the annals of the last century and the century before, and asks what has become of "The Life, once manifest," has his answer when he finds how the arms of temporal power embraced the simple Bride of Christ, as the loving old phrase called the Church. And again he finds it, when he reads how the doctors of the universities bedrugged her and puzzled her.

And, whenever the Life appears, it is as you see a timid snowdrop peeping up amid the frozen ground, or as you hear the song of a frightened bluebird in the midst of the gales of March. The Life is in the simple song of the Moravian brethren. It is as colliers and smiths and hedgers and ditchers meet together at a cross-road, to listen to Wesley. It is as the hunted peasants of the Cevennes defy the trained soldiers of Louis. Always the story is the same. You sought your Lord in a tomb, and you found him in a garden. Man had hewn the tomb. Man had squared the stones. Man had rolled the rock to the door. "But the tomb will not hold him." He stands under the heaven of God with rising sun of morning revealing to you what you do not make out through your tears. It is only when you tear off the cerements of your metaphysics and logic, and swear to God that you will seek only the Life, central and beneath all, that you find your Christian religion as pure and sweet and simple as it always was. It is only when you tear off the ceremonies,—which for their convenience kings and priests have instituted,—and throw them after the grave-clothes, to be fretted by moth, and to find their own place in the ashes, that your faith becomes what it was in the beginning.

The Life was manifested. We have seen it. We have handled it with our hands. He has made clear to us the eternal Life—as it was with the Father.

It is easy to say this at the end of the nineteenth century. It is, thank God, the simplest commonplace to say it. If I spoke of Christians who speak the English language, I might safely say that, from the right wing to the left, every communion of Christians would say to-day that "Christianity is a Life, not a creed or a form." I could cite words to that effect from leading writers of every communion, probably even in the Catholic Church, certainly in all others. But, one hundred years ago, to say that would be heresy. I believe we owe that verbal statement, those particular words, to James Martineau, that great religious philosopher, whose life and work alone would make it an honor to any man to be called an Englishman. But the calm presentation of the truth in language unadorned and unepigrammatic, language simple to baldness, the statement made so definite and clear that men had to accept it, when they hated to,—this proclamation was the work of Channing, the hero of our time, whose birth next week is to celebrate. Mr. Agassiz says of physical discovery, that it always passes through three stages of comment:—

1. Men say it contradicts the Bible.
2. They say they discovered it themselves.
3. They say everybody always believed it everywhere.

Channing's calm enunciation of simple Christianity—that it meant "love God, love man, and live forever," that that is the whole of it—has passed and is passing through just those phases. 1. Men said, it was not in the Bible. 2. Now they all say they discovered it themselves, and—that it is commonplace. Let us thank God for that. The great victory will come when all men everywhere shall say that they always believed it and always will; that there is no intellectual dogma in the Life of Christ; that there is no form of machinery or method requisite to it; that it is simply Life,—the Life of God in the affairs of man.

Less and less shall men seek that life in their plans of salvation, in ingenious tangles of their dialectics.

Less and less shall they seek it in camp or court, by ordered processional or sacrifice.

"Why seek ye the living among the dead?" These are only the blocks which he pushed by. They are the bandages that tied him.

Pardon the blinded believer, if for a moment he do not know the Master whom he thought dead, and who is alive. There needs but one word of living love, and Mary knows him. There needs but a living Church,—ready to speak in his loving spirit,—and the world knows and believes.

Its religion is not a creed: it is not a form. It is the Life of God in the soul of man.

THE NEW BIRTH.

BY JONES VERY.

'Tis a new life; — thoughts move not as they did,
With slow, uncertain steps, across my mind;
In thronging haste fast pressing on, they bid
The portals open to the viewless wind,
That comes not save when in the dust is laid
The crown of pride, — that gilds each mortal brow,
And from before man's vision melting fade
The heavens and earth; — their walls are falling now.
Fast crowding on, each thought asks utterance strong;
Storm-lifted waves swift rushing to the shore,
On from the sea they send their shouts along,
Back through the cave-worn rocks their thunders roar;
And I, a child of God by Christ made free,
Start from death's slumbers to Eternity.

INCREASE OF LIFE.

"Because I live, ye shall live also."—JOHN xiv., 19.

To Jesus Christ, the unseen world and the world which is seen are one world and the same. We talk of "the other world," "the future world," "the world above": he does not speak so. He speaks of heaven as if it were now and here, or might be; and, when they are confused with what he says, it is often because they see double where he sees singly. Nay: when he appears to be confused by what they say, —as sometimes happens,—the best account we can give is that they are talking of this visible world only, while he talks at once of the visible and invisible. There are a hundred texts which show his feeling,— "Lo! I am with you alway, even unto the end of the world." "It is my Father who doeth these works at which you wonder. You do not see him; but, all the same, he is here." "Father, I know that thou hearest me always. I would not have spoken aloud but for the help of these who are standing by." And, when he expresses his trouble because language and metaphor fail him as they do, it is in this very difficulty. Language, having been made by people who rely on their senses, to answer the purposes of the visible and tangible world, breaks down, and breaks down very badly, when it is applied to the range, vastly wider, of that unseen world, which permeates this world, and in which this world floats as a straw floats in the ocean.

Many of you remember our dear friend Starr King's celebrated discourse on "Substance and Shadow." He was at work there to remove exactly this difficulty which the Master tried to remove, nor is there work more essential for the Master's apostle. While we sat and listened to Mr. King, we felt and knew what Jesus teaches. The things which endure are faith and hope and love. Life is the substance, the hard-pan foundation, from which these forms and things around us are born. We cannot see life, nor handle it nor smell it nor hear it nor taste it. But life is; and without it nothing can even appear to be. In the beginning is the Word. Mr. King made us wonder that we had cared so much for this or that little thing, which is but a bubble tossed on the eternal ocean. For the moment, you said you would not be so fooled again. You would take fast hold on love, which you found to be a reality. You would live in hope, or in the infinite world, seeing that is the real world. You would trust wholly in God, seeing all being is from him; and these little things that perish in the using should fall into their own inferior place in your regard or thought or action. While that mood lasted, you caught the true Christian notion of life.

There are not two lives,—a life of heaven there and a life of earth here. These two lives are one life. As the Lord's Prayer says, "God's will is done on earth as it is in heaven." This opens out the meaning of the more figurative phrase, "The kingdom of God is at hand."

The knowledge, that life is indeed larger than the little world we see, grows upon us in a thousand ways. The charm, always new, of watching a baby's life, rests in our interest in the steps of such growth. The little thing first learns its own hands, that they are its own. A little more, and it knows its mother's face, and that she also is its own. By and by, its world enlarges; and at last it knows the whole nursery, which seems a universe indeed, while it is a novelty, so much larger than the petty world the child was in before.

Such steps as these are really enlarging our life all the time afterward, though we do not perhaps note them with quite such eager curiosity. But it is just such a step, when the school-boy, who but yesterday was first in his class and could talk of nothing but the ambitions of the school-room, finds himself the smallest boy in a great mercantile house, where his existence is hardly suspected and nobody knows his name. He learns, by hard rubs perhaps, that the world is much larger than he thought. Yet his chief, the very "grand Cyrus" of them all, the master of masters, has to learn the same lesson. He takes his holiday on some favorable year, he crosses the ocean, he has or thinks he has some business with one of the merchant lords of London or of Paris; and, when the interview has been arranged, after some negotiation, he finds that he was never heard of before, that now his name is forgotten, that there are perhaps a hundred others waiting for their turn, and that he, the first tradesman in his own county, may be yet a very small person in the larger world. So in the world of politics, in the world of literature, in the ambitions of fashion and society, precisely because we are infinite beings,—beings whose nature cannot be limited,—we find all the time that there is far more outside of us in life than we have ever yet attained to. We cannot often enough say that life gives us more, nature gives us more, the more we take. Yes, and the more life gives or nature gives, the more they offer.

The robin in its nest looks into a world made up of a few leaves and boughs around. As the feathers of its wings grow, it flutters a little from the branch, and is astonished to find that the orchard is so large. The bird of passage, when the instinct bred by the season carries it far north or far south, learns that the covert of a few trees, orchard or grove, was nothing to this larger world. Man, of all animals, compasses the whole globe; and then man, in turn, studies the universe outside of it, and finds that this world is a speck, and only a speck, in that universe of whose laws he finds out more and more every day, for they are not beyond the ken of a child of God.

The village boy growing to manhood finds that he is a member of the State as well as of the village. He does not lose his interest in the baseball club or the singing-class, because he has gained an interest in the politics of the State, or is at work for the State Fair, or has been chosen to the Legislature. Then a great crisis comes upon him, and his life enlarges again. Sumter is fired on, and he takes a commission from the President, and enters the service of the nation. Still, he belongs to the village, and to the State. His life as a citizen of the State does not cease because he is an officer of the nation. Such is the illustration of the common life,—life here and life in heaven,—which Jesus Christ is always trying to make us comprehend, even by symbols which he owns are inadequate. You do live in Chester Square or in Union Park; but you also live in Massachusetts, and have duties and pleasures which to that life belong. More than this, you are a citizen of the United States, and as such have other duties and relations. Nay: even if you do not cross oceans or continents, you are also a citizen of the world, and as such have a life yet larger. More than this, says the Saviour of men, you live in heaven, and have relations, pleasures, and duties, as a child of God, as a child of heaven. They are not apart from to-day's duties or pleasures. Rather they are all knit in with them. Nor are they the life of a to-morrow, unattainable until to-day is done with. They are the life of to-day, all mixed in with life which is visible and tangible. A woman's new life—when her first child is in her arms, wholly dependent on her—is, or may be, simply the life of a ministering angel. She does not care for herself, save as she cares for the child which depends on her. Her question is not, "Is the room too hot for me?" but, "Is it too hot for him?" It is not, "What will entertain me?" but, "What will entertain him?" That measure of love is no more perfect in the ministry of an angel than it is in the ministry of any mother who surrenders herself to her child. So of the loyal, absorbed faith of a soldier going into battle. It is not, "Shall I best shelter myself here?" but, "How shall I best protect the men?" It is not, "Shall I get through easiest thus?" but, "How shall I best serve the cause?" No angel or archangel in any hierarchy of God can surpass that loyalty to a cause. And such faith as that, where it exists, manifests the law, the purpose, the system of God's own heaven. Such love as that mother's, such faith as that soldier's, are not to be spoken of as like the heavenly qualities: they are the heavenly qualities. What Jesus is trying to make us see is that heaven thus has its part and place in the world of time, and may wholly master it, if we will. To borrow a striking figure which I once heard Dr. Bush employ, the earth is as full of heaven as a sponge is full of water. Every pore is saturated and crowded with it. And the true child of God, who knows his own dignity, is not forever distinguishing between the sponge and what it holds, between things of time and things of eternity. How can he discriminate? Both are God's work. Both are in God's order. He can sweep a floor to God's glory as well as sing a psalm to his glory. As the true citizen does his duty, and does it of course and without question, never stopping to say, I do this as a Charlestown man, or I do this as a Massachusetts man, or I do this as an American, or this as a citizen of the world, but knows and feels that the one relation belongs to the other, reinforces it, and gains strength from it, just so the child of God lives his earthly life and his heavenly life at once and together. He does not define, nor dissect, nor analyze. There is no separation nor distinction. He speaks at once with the tongues of men and of angels.

He does the deed at once of earth and of heaven. He does his own will, —yes, and he does his Father's will in the same act. For he has so wrought out the divinity of his own nature that his life is hid in God's life. Of which union the perfect statement was made, when Jesus said, "I and my Father are one." For which also he prayed for us, when we prayed that we might be one, as they two are one.

Careless people sometimes express surprise when they find the same man exhibiting what they call the most opposite characters, that he is at once so practical and so ideal. Mr. Emerson, for instance, idealist of the idealists, teaches the most obdurate common-sense in the homeliest Saxon dialect. So Professor Peirce, one who could weigh one comet against another in his scales, who could count the oscillations of the rays of the Pleiades and untangle the cords of the attractions of Orion, was, through and through, an idealist, never so much at home as when he spoke of the foundations of ethics, and in most weighty phrase, rendered homage to the truth. It is only careless people who are so surprised. Earth being all full of heaven, the surprising thing would be if this were not so. The man really practical will be thoroughly ideal. The child of God truly heavenly will deal with things of time as simply and as certainly as God does. Here in your Gospels is Matthew, whom you call and call rightly a man of affairs, tax-gatherer, merchant, —gives you your parables of usury, and buying and selling and all practical affairs. Yes; and it is he who writes down your beatitudes, with that mystic, "Blessed are the pure in heart, for they shall see God." It is he who writes, "Fear not, little flock, it is your Father's good pleasure to give you the kingdom." It is he who sings, shall I say the eternal song of welcome: "Come unto me, ye that labor and are heavy-laden; and I will give you rest. Take my yoke upon you, and learn of me; for I am meek and lowly of heart, and ye shall find rest to your souls." So easily and certainly does a child of God find the eternal truth, and speak it, in the midst of earth's affairs.

Film by film, shred by shred, this child of God lays off one and another of the environments which fetter him. The baby is not held longer in his mother's arms: he totters alone. At last, he is master of the house, and may roam where he will. Nay, the day comes when the doubtful mother must let him run out-doors under his own control. He grows to youth or manhood, and makes his own home. Not even orders from father or mother rule him longer. Perhaps he passes from land to land, acquires the sway of new languages, and is not bound even to one country. Perhaps his word controls other men. What he writes is read by all thinkers, what he thinks is applied in all laws. Perhaps he startles a generation of sleepers, and they take up their beds and walk. All this steady enlargement of life and power is certain, because he is God's child. The soul in him controls muscle, nerve, sense, fibre, blood-vessels, and brain. The God in him controls the organic frame of an earthly tabernacle. One step more, and the sweet singer, who yesterday wrote some psalm of praise for a few companions, casts off this earthly house of a mortal tabernacle, and joins in the chorus of a nobler and larger worship.

The careful reasoner who, with the little tricks of two or three earthly algebras, untangled the problems of the universe, drops off the house of an earthly tabernacle, sees as he is seen and knows as he is known, and rejoices in the untangled heavenly verities. The faithful friend, who let no hour pass unless he had ministered to this orphan, had braced up yonder hesitant. had lifted him who was fallen, or comforted her who was starving, casts off this frail house of an earthly tabernacle; and lo! infinite resource with which to minister, no lack of time for endeavor, and no grinding burden of fatigue. She who, for months and years, lay gently on the sick-bed, who received from one and another a thousand tender ministrations to her pain, and repaid them all in her thankful patience,—she casts off this frail house of this earthly tabernacle; and lo! with the same love, with the same patience, with the same gratitude, she is ministering to them and to ten thousand more, in this glad freedom of disembodied life. As the baby passes into the boy, the boy into the youth, the youth into the man, so, in one more change, not unlike these others, the child of God stands free in the untrammelled life of heaven.

The revelation of life in Jesus Christ is not simply the fact of his personal re-appearance after death. Before he died, he had quickened the life of the world, renewed it, enlarged it. "I am the resurrection and the life: whoso liveth and believeth in me shall never die." Whoever lives with that control of sense and organ by the living soul which to the Christian man is possible, whoever rises superior to pain, hunger, want, whoever lives with the divine life of a son of God, that man knows he does not die. The answer falls fitly on the wretched plaint of Martha, dissatisfied, as well she might be, with the faith of her country and of her time. She sobs out her doleful creed: "I know that he shall rise again, at that distant resurrection, at that last day, which is, oh, so wretchedly far away!" How often has that mournful plaint of that Jewish woman been repeated by persons who have been taught the same Eastern doctrine of a suspended animation, even in Christian churches! Christ will have none of it. "Dead! Do you think I shall die? You believe in me! Do you think any child of God dies? If he once learns to live, if he live in the large life,—the life that believes, that loves, that hopes,—he knows he cannot die."

It is indeed a faith which it needs such as Jesus to instill. Those who knew him took it in and made it real. For us, we drink at the same fountain. The promise was not an empty promise; and when the moment comes, when the cloud opens and the heaven reveals itself, the Comforter, who is the Holy Spirit, speaks to us. Nor is it any new doctrine. It is the word which spoke from the beginning. The Comforter speaks to say that the world of God is larger than this world of man. The life of God is larger than this life, hemmed in by the powers of five senses only, and unable to know more or to do more. The Father of perfect love is always training us for that larger life and those fuller powers. Sometimes he shows us that this is possible. When he calls the careful thinker who has exhausted earthly processes, or the brave leader who has quickened a thousand thousand lives, nay, the loving boy who has shown me what the kingdom of heaven is and what it is like, or the unselfish mother whose life has been all made up of help and blessing to those around her,—when God lifts these into a life unembodied, and therefore unseen, he teaches me again the lesson which Jesus was teaching always. Such lives have larger sphere and duty; for God's purpose is larger than these cramped places and these passing hours. Who lives as they have lived, and with such faith as their faith, these never die.

THE LAW OF CHANGE.

BY JOHN STERLING.

While under heaven's warm evening hues
   They felt their eyes and bosoms glow,
They learned how fondly fancy views
   Fair sights the moment ere they go;

And then, while earth was darkening o'er,
   While stars began their tranquil day,
Rejoiced that Nature gives us more
   Than all it ever takes away.

In earliest autumn's fading woods,
   Remote from eyes, they roamed at morn,
And saw how Time transmuting broods
   O'er all that into Time is born.

The power which men would fain forget—
   The law of change and slow decay—
Came to them with a mild regret,
   A brightness veiled in softening gray.

CONSIDER THE LILIES.

"Consider the lilies, how they grow."—MATT. vi, 28.

THEY do not grow in any spasm of sudden resolution. They seem to wake up, after long indifference. They seem to rush eagerly to light and air, to burst into blossom as quickly as they can, and then to die. But the truth is that all last year they were collecting and digesting from rain and sunshine and air the material which they use in all this outburst. If the bulb had not done its underground duty then, if all nature in union had not done its work then,—if the sun had not shone, the world turned on its axis and flown through space, if the heavens had not clouded and cleared, and raindrops formed and fallen,—there would be no lily to-day. The lily does not have to toil. It does not have to spin. Worlds have moved to and fro that it might blossom, rocks have been ground to powder by glacier and by the tooth of time, soils have been drifted hither and thither as ages have passed by, that the lily might have a place to stand, might have food to digest, might have beauty and fragrance for your delight. What the lily has done or has been in all this infinite movement is this. It has accepted the universe. It has waited for its time, and then has pushed its germ to the sky and its rootlets into the soil. It has not tried to be a law unto itself, or to live and blossom and have a being or some system of its own.

Such hint, at least for our own lives, do we gain when we consider the lilies, how they grow. This is the hint which the Saviour meant to give. Eager as he is that you and I shall recognize the present God, shall gain from his presence just the comfort and strength that he did, shall live and move and have our being in him, he asks us to consider the lilies; for they are trusting God, are obeying the great law of nature in which they have their place and their duty. On the one hand, they do not exaggerate their duty. Therefore, their days are not made wretched by toil. They do their part. On the other hand, they do not sulk nor compel attendant slaves to clothe them in such robes as the servants of Solomon brought him. They do their part, but that part is not toil. It is not abject. It is clear enough that the lily enjoys its life with all the heart and soul it has. It does its little part gladly, and from the Infinite Love and Infinite Beauty it accepts the rest. Here is our lesson.

In the great jubilee of spring-time, which with us takes form as Easter, and which takes some fit form in all religious systems, men do not simply celebrate the new life of the world. They are sure to add to that recognition their praise of the beauty and glory of the world. It is that feeling which heaps up your roses on the communion table, and brings to me in the pulpit here the annual glory of my pansies and the sweet, timid blush of my blood-root. Scepticism has found, in our time, a coarse and hard reply to the statement that the firmament shows God's hand-work. "You must not say that, because the world is, God is." This is the statement. "For if the world were not, you would not be, and you could not be arguing. This is what has happened to survive, under the law of selection, in which no one selects." But no such reply annoys me, no such doubt perplexes me, when I have in my hand a spring anemone, or a sweet violet, or the lily of the field. The world could have existed without either of them. The great dice-box of Destiny could have flung out its worlds into space, with no fragrant violet, with no wind-blown anemone, with no lily of the field, and the balance of gravitation would still have been perfect, the world would have rushed without fragrance and beauty wildly through space. When in the same blossom my eye now revels in color, when I find exquisite form and perfect grace, as I enjoy the fragrance with the color and the form, you find it hard to persuade me that this is the survival of the fittest. When I find the dice always turn up triplets, I am sure that some conscious Power loaded them. Whatever power made rose and lily, and violet and anemone, had the sense of beauty and knew what my sense of beauty would be. So that I find the exquisite rhodora waiting for me in the wilderness, I say gladly,—it is my spontaneous thought,—"The self-same Power that brought me here brought you."

I think I have told the story here of one of my college teachers who joined me one evening in Cambridge, when I was returning from some long tramp, with full store in my tin box of wild flowers which had been opening for me and waiting for me. With an air of reproach, the learned man said to me that he wished he also knew something of flowers, but that, when he was of my age, he was wholly occupied in the care and cure of his soul, and had no heart or time for such things. "Now I have all that settled," he said, with some self-respect, "I wish I knew something of botany."

I was too young, and I trust too modest, to reply. But I know now, what I suspected then, that that man was a fool. I know now that I could have put my soul into no better training than it would gain in a fresh walk under God's open sky, while I was exulting in the dainty delicacy of his work and enjoying the lavish exuberance of the love which cares for all of us. True, I had gone for my flowers from "native impulse." I had never analyzed my motive nor made it matter of study. I went because I wanted to. I liked to do that much more than I liked to read Bickersteth's *Christian Student* or Doddridge's *Rise and Progress*, which my friend would have wished me to be reading. And I believe, what I do not pretend to prove, that that native joy came to me thus, because the Power that put the flowers here put me here, because his life is in all his works, and that his children, of whom I am one, come closer to him as they know more and more of his handiwork and enjoy what he enjoys, as they watch the present life in which his creatures live and move and have their being. I say the present life in which they are now growing. God is: his name is I Am. It is not perhaps easy to think of him as acting now, with just the thought and feeling with which the poet says he acted in the beginning, when God said, "Let the earth bring forth grass." But it ought not to be impossible. God now says, "Let the earth bring forth grass." He *is* saying it at this instant; and, because he *is* saying it at this instant, the earth *is* bringing forth grass at this instant. Just the same creation *is* going forward now which, for convenience of language, we say *went* forward then, in what, for convenience of language, we call the beginning. Perhaps one feels this present power of a present God a little more vividly when one sees it in an unaccustomed way. I have told the story here of one of our first men of science, of whom it would be fair to say that he experienced religion,—though not for the first time, indeed,—when he first put his eye to the eye-piece of a compound microscope of high power. In that moment, he was a witness, at least, of the present work of God,—seeing crystals shape themselves, seeing cells enlarge and double and separate, seeing growth in what seems to be its origin. In truth, there is nothing more remarkable when I see an atom, just now invisible, choose its conscious course and work its way across a tiny drop, than there is when I see an eagle mount in the sky, poise himself in mid-heaven, and plunge in the deep below. In both cases, I see an exertion of spontaneous will; and that is always unexplainable. But, when I see this through the microscope, the sight shocks my dead habit; and I feel that God is now as he was in the beginning, and as he ever will be, world without end.

"I Am is thy memorial still." Fortunately for me, I said something like this in preaching in England two years ago; and, fortunately for me, one of the first naturalists of our time happened to hear me. He was kind enough to stop after the service and introduce himself to me, and make an appointment with me, that with my eyes I might see some of these marvels in a world which in our language is small, while in other languages it may be as great as to us is the world of Arcturus and of Orion. Of the marvels which that day he showed me, that which I find stands out in my memory most distinctly is the home which a little creature builds for itself from specks of quartz sand at the depth of about a mile beneath the surface of the ocean. Of these little creatures there are thousands of varieties. When their spring-time comes to them in their dark home, whatever that spring-time may be, these little creatures build for themselves their houses or their nests, each in his fashion, just as the sparrow builds his nest in one fashion under my piazza, and the hang-bird builds his in my elm-tree in another. To speak only of one of them, whose house I saw from every point of view, he chooses to select for its material only the finest quartz sand, from the varied material of the bottom of the ocean. The whole house, when it is done, is about the size of the head of the smallest pin. For this there are needed something like one million atoms of the sand. These atoms are formed in a perfect sphere, with a little neck at the top, like the short, open neck of a flask. The atoms are of every conceivable shape, and precisely resemble under the microscope the stones in a wall in a New England pasture. And precisely as a skilful workman will fit those stones together, so that the cracks between them shall be the smallest possible, precisely as he makes one side of his wall smooth or flat, while he is indifferent to the other side, and leaves it jagged and uneven, so does this little creature work, in building the little gourd-shaped bottle which is his home. The outside is as smooth as possible, the inside is rough, as might happen from the shape of the stones he handled. How much the little creature knows I cannot tell. But, like the lily, he knows the law of the universe in which he lives: he makes himself a part of that universe, he accepts its conditions and does his share. I believe he does it consciously. I believe he does it because he wishes to do it. If he does, he also is a fellow-workman together with God.

I grant the exceeding difficulty of thinking, feeling, believing, and seeing that God is a spirit. I am afraid that difficulty will yet last for generations. The woman felt it at Sychar, when Jesus said, "God is a Spirit"; and her brothers and sisters have felt it ever since, and will continue to feel it for a long time. Even the language of the best books does not always help us. Thus, the Bible language and the hymns drawn from it often run back to the child's notion, which was the earlier Jewish notion, that God lives in a particular place, that he waits for this message, and that he sends that angel. But, in this great business which is central, everything makes one hopeful now. All science shows more and more one law in all space and in all time. Whatever Power made this world, the same Power sustains it, made and sustains Arcturus and Orion. To this Power there is no such limitation as Space, there is no such limitation as Time. Now, about this Present Power, you may have two notions. According as you have one notion, you may call it "It," and say, "It does not know what it is doing." Or you may call this power "He," and you may say, "He does know what he is doing." In this last case, you accept the religious philosophy of Jesus Christ. As you consider the lilies, you see in them the tokens of God's present love and of his present wish that this world among other worlds may be beautiful and happy. To take Miss Fuller's phrase, which I used before, you "accept the universe." To take the quaint phrase of the catechism, you "enjoy God." Best of all, perhaps, is the phrase of the parable,—you "enter into the joy of your Lord."

I certainly am not going to argue in five minutes this great question, whether the Power which sustains this universe is He or is It; whether He be conscious of his work or not. Indeed, I do not think that question will ever be solved by argument. Rather, I believe that a world of the conscious children of this God steadily moves forward and upward to its own solution of the question, and with every day, indeed, of the world's life, knows him more and knows him better. "Nearer, my God, to Thee, nearer to Thee." In this great issue, I like Dr. George Putnam's epigram. "You say that all this beauty, wisdom, tenderness, harmony, are the result of certain laws of matter, which you tell me are one law. I accept your conclusion. I believe what you say, only with a little change of language. If Matter can do such wonders as these, wonders which in my highest spiritual flight I enjoy and prize, I find it better to call it Spirit. What you call Matter I call Spirit." Or, as a matter of statement, I have found many people are helped by Freeman Clarke's simple statement, which I wish I could repeat in his own clear language. "You say that this exquisite human organization in which a million million cells of being coöperate with each other for one aim has resulted in the marvel of thought, in the marvel of conscious being, and in the greater marvels of faith and hope and love. You tell me it is possible for a bit of mechanism to be so exquisitely perfect that the result is conscious life; as if the beautiful organ yonder were so marvellously formed that of itself, without direction, it should begin, when it chose, to play a symphony more marvellous than Beethoven ever dreamed of, and, when it chose, should cease and be still. Very well. If mechanism can thus rise to consciousness in man, why may not the mechanism and harmony of your universe rise to consciousness as well? Why might not all the stars of the morning sing together, when they heard all the sons of men shouting for joy?" I acknowledge that these are not arguments: they are simply statements in language, by two clear-headed men, not apt to deceive themselves in a matter where they would not argue. I quote them, because I think what is needed most is to rescue the language in which we speak of

God, the Infinite Spirit, from the language in which children might speak, or savages,—the language of idol worshippers or of those who imprison God in a visible form. Let me just say this, and it shall be all. There is to me something amazing in that presumption which I meet now and then in the reviews, which really supposes that the thousand million men, more or less, who live in visible bodies in this little world, are the only conscious beings in the infinite universe. It was absurd enough, in the days of men's ignorance, to suppose that sun, moon, planets, and stars all circled around this little globe of ours,— absurd enough to suppose that sun and moon were set only to give us light, and that stars were set in constellations only that men might exult in their beauty. But this absurdity is nothing to the arrogant insolence of the presumption which tells me that, while I am conscious of my existence here and look back with interest on my past and with curiosity on my future, the Power which makes me and sustains me, orders the sun to paint the lily for me and bids the lily grow to be painted, is not conscious of his past, is not conscious of his present work, and is not curious about his future. This arrogance reaches its climax, when we are told, as we so often are, that we men, forsooth, who are the lords of creation, are indeed its only conscious inhabitants,—so many Alexander Selkirks, indeed, stranded on the edge of a desert.

"I am monarch of all I survey.
My reign there is none to dispute."

But I did not ask you to consider the lilies, that I might engage in this high argument which is, as I suppose, beyond logical reasoning. I wanted to say enough, this morning, shall I say, to justify our instinctive passion for flowers, and gardening, and nature, and the woods. I want to do honor to that nerve of the eternal life which runs through it all, and makes its joy part, indeed, and element of the joy of God. This is no poor bit of the pleasure of sense alone. The passion that takes you out of doors is not one of the vulgar, selfish, or personal passions which Puritans were right in holding under lock and key. Here is the child of God who wants to know what his Father is doing. His own life quickens and warms and grows young as days grow longer and the sun rides higher, and it is in his godly nature and by one of the divine laws that he delights to see how other creatures of God are breaking from their wintry prison. Life seeks life and loves life. In the opening of a catkin of a willow, in the flight of the butterfly, in the chirping of a tree-toad or the sweep of an eagle, my life loves to see how others live, exults in their joy and so far is partner in their great concern. And this is really what we mean when we say, what I think people generally understand, that a man is apt to be nearer to God when he is out of doors than when he is in his home. Literally, this might not be true. But what we are after is the larger Life. We do not want to be limited wholly by things of the flesh, what we shall eat, what we shall drink. After these things, the Gentiles seek, the Philistines, most of all. What we do need is more of God. It may be some sudden and new hint of him, it may be the infinite and perpetual lesson of the ocean or of the stars. Always it is Life,—life larger than a room, life larger than a day. It was when he got outside a room that the first man, in the cool of the day, walked with God. And for us, in these later days, it is that we may walk with God, more and more often, that the Saviour bids us " consider the lilies."

LUTHER'S EASTER HYMN.

In the bonds of Death He lay
    Who for our offence was slain;
But the Lord is risen to-day,
    Christ hath brought us life again.
Wherefore let us all rejoice,
Singing loud with cheerful voice,
        Hallelujah!

Of the sons of men, was none
    Who could break the bonds of Death;
Sin this mischief dire had done;
    Innocent was none on earth,
Wherefore Death grew strong and bold,
Would all men in his prison hold.
        Hallelujah!

Jesus Christ, God's only Son,
    Came at last our foe to smite,
All our sins away hath done,
    Done away Death's power and might.
Only the form of Death is left,
Of his sting he is bereft,
        Hallelujah!

That was a wondrous war, I trow,
    When Life and Death together fought,
But Life hath triumph'd o'er his foe,
    Death is mock'd and set at naught.

LUTHER'S EASTER HYMN.

'Tis even as the Scripture saith,
Christ through death has conquer'd Death;
    Hallelujah!

    The rightful Paschal Lamb is He,
        On whom alone we all must live,
    Who to death upon the tree,
        Himself in wondrous love did give.
Faith strikes His blood upon the door.
Death fell, and dares not harm us more.
        Hallelujah!

    Let us keep high festival
        On this most blessed day of days,
    When God his mercy showed to all;
        Our Sun is risen with brightest rays,
And our dark hearts rejoice to see
Sin and night before Him flee.
        Hallelujah!

    To the supper of the Lord,
        Gladly will we come to-day;
    The word of peace is now restored,
        The old leaven is put away.
Christ will be our food alone.
Faith no life but His doth own.
        Hallelujah!

EASTER.

"Because I live, ye shall live also."—JOHN xiv, 19.

THE Sects in the church might be judged by a comparison of their favorite holidays. And so might eras in history be judged. It is matter of real interest, then, to see how all poets and prophets of all divisions of the Church unite on this day, to proclaim it the Sunday of Sundays, the High Holy Day of the year. For this is to say that poet and prophet, of every sect and those least sectarian, have found out at last that the Christian Religion stands for Life. Life instead of form; Life instead of Laws; Life instead of Grave-clothes; Life instead of Tombs; Life instead of Death;—that is what Christianity means, and what it is for. You would be tempted to say that the Saviour had already enforced this completely in what he *said* to men; tempted to say that Easter morning was not needed either for illustration or enforcement. Certainly the gospel texts are full of the lesson. "Because I live, ye shall live also." "As the Father hath life in himself, so hath he given to the Son to have life in himself." "This is Life Eternal—to believe on thee." And central text of all, the text we have chosen for the motto of this church, "I have come that they might have life, and that they might have it more abundantly." If texts alone ever did anything, these and a thousand more would show what The Truth is, and The Way. But one is tempted, in bitter moods, to say that texts never do anything, that words never achieve or finish anything. One is tempted to remember how he said that any man who prepared God's way is greater than any man who only proclaims it, how prophets and prophesying were done with, mere talk was over—praise the Lord! and energy, action, force had come in instead, praise the Lord! Yet, if anybody did still trust in talk, he might take a lesson from these Gospels.

Here are all these people, high and low, on tenter-hooks of excitement and curiosity. What has this man to teach? Where will that man take us? " What is this Judas the Gaulonite after? What has that Edomite to propose? What will Theudas promise?" John Baptist comes in. "Who is he? Is he Elijah? Has he any plan? Has he any word? There is a Nazarene up at Capernaum. Nobody ever talked like him, and he has made a blind man see. Let us go and find him." They come swarming up around him, block the streets, block the roads, press over the houses where he is at meat, to ask him what he proposes.

What *does* he propose? Life! That those who are dead shall live. That people shall pray for themselves, who have been praying by proxy. That people shall pray where they are, who have been going to Jerusalem to worship. That people shall do themselves what they have been expecting others to do. That people shall enter heaven now, which they have been supposing should wait for them after ages of æons. God is yours, Heaven is yours, if you would only Live. Why, if you had as much life in you as this grain of mustard seed has, you would share God's own power, and live in God's own heaven! For God is Here, and God is Now. The kingdom of heaven is at hand. Life! That is what he proposes.

These words, even dimly echoed, shake the ages. If words alone were worth much, you would say that they must have touched to the heart the men who heard them, the women and the children. I do not say, but in a fashion, they did touch them. But what appeared on the surface was, that when he said some such words, this group of his hearers would say, " Can't you show us a miracle, as you showed the people of Nain?" and that set of people would say, " Can't you feed us here on the grass, as you fed us last week by the lake-side?" and these near friends would say, " Cannot you make me Senator and cannot you make me a Publican, when you come into your kingdom, and have offices to fill?" " *Life!* Yes, that sounds all very well in sermons, and when one is making a platform, but, as between friends, other things are to be considered." So that, so far as appears, the applause of the multitudes, and the crowded streets of Capernaum, of Tiberias and of Jericho, never advanced the real kingdom by the breadth of one hair.

I do not think it would be fanciful, as it certainly would not be difficult, to describe the different set of people among those who surrounded him, who, from one prejudice or other, or from one or another one-sidedness, missed the reality, *Life*, and took from him and his words something less which they could have taken from earthen vessels.

1. There were mere sentimentalists, who were so passionately in love with him, that they must be always kissing the hem of his garment, or sitting in his shadow. They were worthless when he was out of sight, they were useless when he sent them on an errand. If he said firmly, "I must go away," they were not simply in tears, they were prostrate and wretched; and when he went away, in truth, it proved that they had not found out what the word "*Life*" means. That type of people exists in the church to this hour.

2. Then there were the "Doctrinaires" shall I call them, the people with the ink-horns and note-books, the "scribes and lawyers." They knew what he said on the second day of Nisan, and they could compare it with what he said on the "second Sabbath after the First." "I tell you he said, 'He that is not against us is on our side.' I have it written down here." "I don't care for that, he certainly said, 'He that is not with me is against me.' He said it, that day we ate our lunch by the tamarisk tree. Here are my notes." "I am sure he said, 'A prophet is without honor except in his own country,' here are the words." "What do I care for your words? Perhaps you do not read your notes right. Now mine are perfectly plain. 'A prophet is not without honor, except in his own country.' He said it to Simon the Smith, when we met him at Bethany." These are the people who lost sight of Life in the Letter. The same type of people exist in the church to-day. Jesus tried to silence them, but he did not silence them by what he said of jots and tittles. Paul tried to do the same, when he said, "The Letter killeth, and the Spirit giveth Life." If words had been worth more we should never have heard of them again.

3. Then there was another set of people, whom I might call the imitative people, who were very precise about method. "Did you see John Baptist with him at the Jordan? Then you can tell us all about it? How deep did they go into the water? Did John take his hand, or did he take a shell, when he baptized him?" "You are quite sure that he did not wash his hands before he went into Matthew's dinner party?" "Yes, quite sure." "Remember that, Salome, he did not wash

his hands, be sure you remember." " Are you sure he ate quail on the Fast-day?" " I am perfectly sure, my sister saw him." " You are sure it was not after sun-down?" " After sun-down? Oh, no! the sun was an hour high." " Remember, Salome, could you not write it down? The sun was an hour high." " You say they rubbed the corn in their hands?" " Certainly they rubbed it in their hands." " Had they no linen cloth to rub it in?" " No. There was no cloth at all." " Salome, write that down. Corn eaten on the Sabbath day is not to be rubbed in a linen cloth, it is to be rubbed in the hands."

These are the people who lose Life in their anxiety for form. You see I do not exaggerate. Just that class of Christians, such as they are, exist to-day, and make up large sections of the church, if we could believe, as, thank God, we cannot, the technical classifications.

In the midst of all this folly, Jesus moved as simply and as omnipotently as Orion moves across a winter sky, careless of cloud, careless of gust of snow, careless of smoke or dust, careless of whirlwinds. If people see him, well ; if they do not see him, so much the worse for them. No matter, he is the same. Let them take or make this lesson or that lesson, he is the same. Life and Eternal Life—that is what he stands for. God with Man. The Eternal Life of the Unchanging God in the Human Form and in the midst of Earth's surroundings!

Yes, my friends, and so we ask naturally, " Do we see him?" But even that is of no consequence, he tells us, in comparison with this. " Are we alive?" Nay, that question itself deceives us. Are we even sure that we know what the word Life means? There is a description, somewhere, of the new emotion, the new senses, the new joy, the wild, strange surprise, with which an imaginative man, new-made, saw sunrise and its glories, drank in the freshness of morning and the luxury of day for the first time, ready to sing as Adam sang,

"These are thy glorious gifts, Father of all."

" How could it be for the first time?" says some Nicodemus. " Could he enter again into his mother's womb and be born?" It *was* for the first time, because in the reckless habits of those days in Kentucky, where this man lived, he could not remember till now the night when he had not gone to sleep the worse for liquor, so that he could not remember till now the morning when he had waked fresh and pure and able to enjoy.

Not till now, when some apostle of the Word of God had made him fling off that old bondage and enabled him in that one detail of life, to see, and feel, and hear, and understand. Now that man, till that miracle was wrought, did not know what the word *morning* meant. His definition of it was inadequate. His sense of it was all incomplete. If he had talked with a true artist about it, or a simple child, or a pure woman, he would not have known what the words meant which they used. He would have said they were talking rhetoric, that they were exaggerating, "that they were lying to him." He would always have said this, till the blessed moment when he was born again so that he could see for himself, and hear and know and understand. And that fatuity and ignorance is only a little type or illustration, in a single detail, of our inability from ignorance to use the word Life at all, in the sense in which Jesus used it, until and unless we have boldly entered into Life, as he said to the young gentleman of Edom. There is no "book of the opera" of Life which will tell you how charming it is to see it. There is no transparency in front of the show, which will answer the purpose for you to look upon. You must push the door open and go in. There is no way in which you can read the play, and feel it and understand it, as if you had been one of the actors. No! It is to no such sham or imitation that your Father invites you. "Here is my home," he says, "come into my house." "Here is my feast," he says, "come sit at my feast." "Here is Life Eternal. Oh, my children, because you are my children, *Live* while you live."

That is what God says to us, by every voice of his. It is what he says this day, of all days, by his son, Well Beloved. What we say, is of little consequence. But what we determine and do, is of great consequence to ourselves, if to nobody beside! It is as nothing to us whether we see the risen Saviour or not. Many who did see him did not profit by what they saw. It is as nothing to us, whether we believe he were Son of God, if all this time we are acting as if we were not God's children. To state this in the familiar words of the Old Theology, one of the most distinguished Baptist preachers a few weeks since described the incarnation of God in Christ, with intense earnestness, and therefore intense power. Then, to the great assembly, which followed him eagerly in his demonstration that God was in the flesh—

speaking to the world by Christ Jesus—he said, "This is nothing to you unless you dare say this day that God is Incarnate in you." Perfectly true! The Resurrection miracle is nothing to you and me, if it is only an event of eighteen centuries by-gone. Unless we can Live the Immortal Life, unless we can receive God to his own Home in these Hearts of ours, the texts are nothing to us unless these daily lives illustrate them. Parable is nothing unless the Good Samaritan bends in these streets over the bleeding traveller; unless in your home, the tender father can receive the returning prodigal! For all that wealth of miracle, of precept and of example was never lived out, merely that we might have one more frieze of old-time ornament to be sculptured on the upper walls of our temples. Miracle was wrought, parable invented, sermon preached, yes, and the cross was borne, that this world might be lifted from the groveling existence of brutes to the nobler life of men: that you and I, that he and she, that all men everywhere might truly Live! And the Festival of to-day, if it is anything but a tawdry lie, or the Great Marvel which it celebrates, if it is anything but an inexplicable curiosity of history, mean both alike, that you and I are pledged anew to-day, and covenant anew to-day, that for us we will live the life of the Living children of a Living God.

To cite another word from another of the great preachers, our neighbor Mr. John Weiss;

"It is one thing to believe in immortality. It is quite another thing to live as an immortal."

This pledge means for a church, that is for an organization of Christian men and women, that it will do what God has to do, in the place where he has planted it. To say it would do what Christ would have done, is only an effort to make the other statement more real. It is his representative. It claims to be God's own beloved child. This church because its Easter Festival is real undertakes this day in the echoes of its music, and before its flowers have withered, to comfort those that mourn, to heal those that are broken-hearted, to open the eyes that are blind, and to speak God's love to those who have not heard it, to proclaim glad tidings indeed, to the poor.

And each child of God here, immortal, never-dying, begins a new life to-day. It is to be a life which enjoys every blessing of God's love. It is to be a life which trusts in his infinite power.

It is to be a life which treads under foot and despises the rags of Cerement which the Earth has worn.

It is to be a life which spends and is spent, in the service of Truth, Holiness, and Love.

It is to be a life in which each man lives for each other man, because each man lives for the purpose of the Living God.

It is a life, therefore, which with every new day, is new born. From every night's sleep it starts as from an Easter Sepulchre. With every new day's opportunities, it steps forward as serene and cheerful as an archangel to his mission. Why worry one's self about the past, about a tomb? Why seek ye the living among the dead? He is not here. He is Risen!

GOOD FROM EVIL.

BY JOHN STERLING.

Thou God, so rulest; such the plan
 Of endless change, evolving good.
Thou leadest thus desponding man
 With hope on all thy works to brood.

In all to see an endless will
 For all educing light and life,
The blessings born from seeming ill
 And peace the end assured of strife.

So thou in me, O God! ordain
 That quiet faith and gladness pure
O'er all convulsions past may reign,
 And root my soul in Thee secure.

So haggard wrecks of former woe
 Beneath thy radiant light may shine,
And charmed to steadfast being show
 O'er all their havoc bliss divine!

THE MIRACLE OF LIFE.

I TRIED last Sunday to state in words the relation, so close, of all Spiritual Being and all Spiritual Life. Words stumble and break down in the effort. But every Religious service is one effort more to express in some way man's certainty of his hold on God, and this is man's certainty that his own Life is allied to the Life of the Universe.

Because this is so, Religious service fails, or is apt to fail, when it occupies itself with things which are not alive. Of course the effort is, to make these things the medium for expressing to God what man would say. Thus the shepherd in Hebron, Abraham's neighbor, has a beautiful lamb or sheep, and he knows that from the love of God and his present care come flock, and grass which feeds the flock, and dew and rain which water the grass, and the daily sunshine which makes the whole rejoice. Because he knows this, and because he is grateful, he brings to the altar this pet lamb and offers it for his sacrifice. It is exactly as the children in a great school might select the best drawings which they had made, or perhaps even write some copies of verses, to send to the benefactor who has endowed the school and has given them power to write or to draw so well. Such is the origin of sacrifice as a method or form of worship. But, as time goes on, as most men do something else than thus take care of sheep or oxen, as in more savage days all men did, the *thing* comes between the child and his Father. The sacrifice does not express life. It rather expresses death, and so that form of worship gives way. You and I would say the same thing of the use of incense in worship. The curling smoke and the pervading odor, in their day seemed to express and so did express what Mr. Montgomery calls

"The motion of a hidden fire
That trembles in the breast."

So far and so long was the use of incense a fit help in worship, and for some people it is so now. But for others, the mechanism of the censer, the swinging of the box, the providing the gums, are but a material matter, and the rite is worthless. Spoken language in worship cannot pretend to be free from the same difficulty. The vibration of the air, which we call sound, is after all a movement of matter. It is possible, therefore, that words, hymns, liturgies and rituals which once lived, which expressed the living love of the living child for the living God, shall become dead because they become mechanical. Mr. Edison would make for us a phonograph which could be run by clock-work and would repeat for us the whole Greek liturgy of St. Andrew or St. James, though there were not a child of God within a hundred miles. And I am afraid that you and I have heard what were called prayers, uttered by the subtler mechanism of the human lips, but which expressed as little of that living love of a living child for a living Father. And so of the central place which music occupies in worship. Music holds that central place because it is infinite on one side, and finite on the other; because it is so far indefinite in the aspiration which it expresses; because each waiting soul can use it almost as he will. From the same strains one life takes comfort, one takes hope, one takes instruction. But music also depends upon these vibrations of the air, and from godless lips and godless hearts and godless lives, music also is but a bit of the mechanism of things.

Now the business of public worship as it is the business of private prayer and communion is to make life more alive. When we come here, or when we go into the closet to pray, it is that the life within us may be stronger to control this mechanism of things. That is to say, Religion must magnify the soul which rules, rather than the body which obeys, must turn to the God who creates whenever she speaks of the world which is created. Because language is material, it is easier to look the other way, and to do the other thing. It is easier for men to look on the dust, from which God made them, and in their vulgar way to talk to death and decay. I do not know what else fills literature with the cheap sensation which is always produced by the coarsest description of a death-bed. I do not know why else even the writers for children gloat over the tales of sickness and other failures of the flesh. For the uses of such writers a dying dog seems better than a living lion. And just as the hateful gossip of a village goes round delighted if she can tell you of the ravages of a new epidemic, and is fairly balked when you can prove to her that the sufferers have recovered, so even the pulpit and the other voices of the church sink into the carnal habit of whining about sin and failure and misery, about sickness and death, about disease of body, mind and soul with a kind of gusto of delight. As if innocence, courage, and virtue, faith, hope and love were not the essential and central subjects of their lessons, to which lapse and disease are only incidental and secondary! In a sectarian newspaper the other day I saw a book criticised as unchristian, because its effort was only to show the Christian victories of faith and hope and love. It seemed, forsooth, that it ought to have told how wretched its hero was before he was converted, and from what depths of misery Christ had saved him. Then, and only then, according to this critic, would it have a truly religious savor.

Against all this heathenism and earth worship, Easter, the Holiday of Life, makes the annual protest; against the habit of considering the machinery; against the microscopic analysis which is satisfied with grovelling in the dust; against the morbid pursuit of studying disease instead of health; against the cloister notion that tears are more virtuous than smiles. Easter day reminds us that the Son of Man was Son of God as well. It reminds us that as God's children *we* have privilege of godly life and godly communion. It lifts us for the day, it would fain lift us for the year, from dwelling among the graves.

The last account given of the successive steps in the history of man's body, suggests that the ancestor of all men now living was probably a Marine Ascidian, which is to say a sea-worm, living in an amphibious life on the edge of the sea, now washed by the rising tide, and then left to try experiments with air. It is supposed that the frame of man, by successive improvements and gradations, has been enlarged and uplifted by that Power which controls the world, till now man stands erect

"And is able to look upon the heavens."

Grant that this is so. At the beginning of this career the sea-worm which you say was our ancestor was alive. There was that life which

THE MIRACLE OF LIFE.

enabled him to wish, to strive, and within the limits of his being to do what he chose. Life, will, choice, desire. These did not come to him from the tides. These were no product of his daily food. They enabled him in his poor way to use the tides, and to purvey for his subsistence. They made him in his way, lord of the earth, the sea, and of mere things. And all your chemistry and all your analysis will never show you what this Life is, which rules over things, and rules them with the absolute empire which every day is witness to. Such are the little types of Life's victory. Even the opening of these flowers is such a type of it; the new carol of the birds of spring is a type of it; the green on the hill-side is a type of it. *Life*, which is inexplicable to the student of things, *life*, which controls and uses things, is asserted in all these spring-time miracles. And when one looks at the noblest victories of all, as when one sees St. Vincent working at the galley oar that he may help the poor slaves who are chained at his side, when one sees Ridley dying at the stake that other men may know what is the truth for which he dies, nay, whenever one reads anything noble, glad, and great in the history of the world, he finds another of the victories which Easter morning commemorates. The victory of the soul over matter. The sway of the Spirit over things. The victory of Life over things which rust and decay. The victory of Life which is Eternal over Death, which is only an aspect of Time and a Delusion.

The joyous celebration of Easter is not simply the commemoration of the rolling away of the rock from the Sepulchre. It is the celebration of every triumph of the Eternal and Infinite soul of man. A celebration, then, well worth cherishing in an age which is a little too proud of its success in raking over dust heaps, and putting labels on the treasures it finds in them. If we enter into the spirit of the celebration it will help us, as I believe George Herbert says, to look upward more in all this new-born year and to look downward less. It will tempt us in the midst of our study of things and our analysis of their forms, to study even with more eagerness the history of man, and the triumphs over things of the living soul, the child of God. Of course we shall be curious about God's handiwork, curious about the palace in which man the immortal lives. But unless we are fools, our interest in the palace, in its carvings, its fret work, its pictures or its dirt and ashes will not so engross us, but we shall look to see and listen to hear if he who inhabits the palace, if the Sovereign, or some prince of the blood Royal, should appear.

It is, for instance, a fascinating study to trace along the history and the rival fortunes of the Races of Men; how certain laws of climate or of blood seem to have compelled the Roman to his destiny, the Greek to his, and the Anglo-Saxon to his. But no one studies those intricacies really, who does not acknowledge that right across their currents, the Omnipotent Life of some infinite child of God comes boldly in, setting up here, pulling down there, and creating history. We prattle about this Race which has achieved this, and that Race which has achieved that, and then are forced to confess that one man, such a man as Abraham, takes the whole destiny of what we call a Race, and uses it as a boy uses a plaything. He diverts it from the course in which it was moving, and bids the history of the world turn another way. In the midst of a luxurious physical and sensual civilization, close to the region where tradition and theory imply that civilization began, this Abraham is born in a race of men, all whose tendencies are beastly. That is, they are governed through and through by physical appetite. Combine the lowest lust of Vienna or Calcutta to-day, with the most wretched sensuality of the tribes of the Amazon, and your picture is not black enough to represent that nature-worship. In the midst of it this one man, Abraham, breaks away. None of it for him! He has spoken to the Unseen Force who rules this universe. And that Force has spoken to him. He will not stay and no family of his shall stay in such filth of debauchery. Westward! to the land God shall show him. The purpose it is, the determination it is, of one man. He will leave them and he will open another volume of history, with another basis and another destiny. Westward he marches. He sets up his altar and pitches his tent. And from that determination of his, that resolution made with prayer and held to by a determined will, the after history of the whole world, as it proves, proceeds. From that determination comes the purer life and nobler being of a race of men who are not governed by appetite, but by the will of the unseen God. From that race of men proceed the laws and institutions which at this hour underlie the civilization of the victorious and successful half of the world. All because one man, conscious of God's being, obeyed God's law as he understood it. The will of that man, the choice of that man, the determination of that man, say simply the Life of that man so prevailed. The Holiday of to-day commemorates such victories.

Such decision, determination, personal power is it which creates the Christian civilization of all our half the world. America once discovered, every fool could say that the voyage was easy. America once discovered, every Vespucius, every Pinzon, every Cabot was willing to make new voyages to the land they knew was there. No rebellious crews now! No wish to turn back to Egypt after the Promised Land has been found. It is just as now every invention has a hundred pirates. A man cannot write a ballad, but he shall start a dozen parodies. But the first Columbus! Ah! there is one of the victories of Life. It is the resolute determination of a child of God which sends him forward. It is not climate that makes him. It is not race that compels him nor destiny. He is his own destiny. He sees through all the westward fogs. He determines. He will carry through. Failure here, failure there, this rebuff, that rebuff,—what are they to an Infinite child of an Infinite God? This thing must be done, shall be done. When the faith and will of such a man speak thus, why, the thing is done. The oceans give a pathway to such a determination and the new world is thrown open to men who know how to use it. A victory of life over things, over physical laws, over what men call fate or destiny!

Yes, and these achievements are only two little parts of the great achievement of history, of the great central day of which this day is the anniversary. The great event of history is in the great miracle of Life: when to a paralyzed world Jesus Christ said, "Take up your bed and walk," and at his voice that world obeyed. The victory of life over death! Why to speak of the mere forms of physical being, it seems that the Roman Empire, whose eagles flaunted in a dying Saviour's face, whose soldiers nailed his body to the cross, was at that very instant dying out in its own lusts. It seems that in the direct result of the chosen lawlessness of its being, the people were dying out of it, because, with its eyes open, it preferred to live for the flesh and sense, and not to live by the spirit and the truth. It seems there were fewer men and women in each century than in the century before. It was to such physical death as that that Jesus Christ spoke the word of more abundant life. And that is only one illustration. It was to such cruelty as permitted parents to kill their own children if they were in the way, it was to such agonies of bleeding hearts as were implied in the worst conceivable system of slavery, it was to such lust in Rome and Athens and Alexandria as repeated the beastly orgies from which Abraham turned in Ur of the Chaldees, it was from these that Jesus Christ bade the world turn and Live; and the world, hearing him, obeyed. It was from the placid satisfaction in which even the Ciceros and the Aureliuses said, as the Platos and even the Socrates of another generation said, that the great mass of the people were to be rated as the brutes, with lives like theirs, and with rights like theirs and with deaths like theirs, that Jesus Christ called noble and plebeian alike, and compelled each to own that the other was his brother and of the same life-blood.

Yes, and such changes in habit, in thought and in society are only the faint dawn of the day. Even in our time, though we see a world which with the lip confesses his empire, we know how hollow is much of the confession. "This people honoreth me with their tongue, but their heart is far from me." We know how in Christian Paris, in Christian London, in Christian New York, in Christian Boston, there is heathenism, which, in its horrid way gives us the suggestions by which we can study that more terrible heathenism of Athens and Rome and Alexandria. Still we have now no fear of the issue. There is a great deal of reconstruction to be done, but the victory is sure, and we know it. We know what Cicero and Aurelius did not know, that in this world, God's Kingdom steadily comes. We know that this Easter day shines on a nobler world than that of a century ago. We know that that Easter was brighter than that of the century before. We know we need no demonstration, that our children's children, a century hence, will look back on the Christian civilization of to-day, amazed indeed, that we should think it worthy of congratulation.

And all this is the victory of Life—yes, of one Life. It is the victory of him who is Lord of Life, of whom that title is the highest title and the proper name. It is not in any physical law of gulf streams, of tidal currents, of simooms, of the world's attractions in its orbit, or of the perturbations in its planetary career that such changes come. They are the victories of the Spirit. They are the conquests of Life. Into this world came that Son of God, who knew God most completely.

And he said, "I have come that this world might have life, and might have it abundantly."

And he lived, and he died, and this day he rose again.

Because he lived, this world begins to live truly. And of its Spiritual birth this day is the anniversary!

EASTER DAY.

BY REV. JOHN KEBLE.

"And as they were afraid, and bowed down their faces to the earth, they said unto them, Why seek ye the living among the dead? He is not here, but is risen."—ST. LUKE, xxiv. 5, 6.

Oh day of days! shall hearts set free
No " minstrel rapture " find for thee?
Thou art the sun of other days,—
They shine by giving back thy rays.

Enthronèd in thy sovereign sphere
Thou shed'st thy light on all the year;
Sundays by thee more glorious break,
An Easter Day in every week;

And week-days, following in their train,
The fulness of thy blessing gain,
Till all, both resting and employ,
Be one Lord's day of holy joy.

Then wake, my soul, to high desires,
And earlier light thine altar fires;
The world some hours is on her way,
Nor thinks on thee, thou blessed day;

Or if she think, it is in scorn;
The vernal light of Easter morn
To her dark gaze no brighter seems
Than Reason's on the Law's pale beams.

EASTER DAY.

"Where is your Lord?" she scornful asks;
"Where is his hire? We know his tasks.
  Sons of a King ye boast to be;
  Let us your crowns and treasures see."

We in the words of truth reply,
(An angel brought them from the sky,)
"Our crown, our treasure, is not here,—
'T is stored above the highest sphere;

"Methinks your wisdom guides amiss,
  To seek on earth a Christian's bliss;
  We watch not now the lifeless stone;
  Our only Lord is risen and gone."

Yet even the lifeless stone is dear,
  For thoughts of him who late lay here;
  And the base world, now Christ has died,
  Ennobled is, and glorified.

No more a charnel-house, to fence
  The relics of lost innocence,
  A vault of ruin and decay;—
  The imprisoning stone is rolled away;

'T is now a cell, where angels use
  To come and go with heavenly news,
  And in the ears of mourners say,
"Come, see the place where Jesus lay;"

'T is now a fane, where Love can find
  Christ everywhere embalmed and shrined;
  Aye gathering up memorials sweet,
  Where'er she sets her duteous feet.

EASTER.

Oh! joy to Mary first allowed,
When roused from weeping o'er his shroud,
By his own calm, soul-soothing tone,
Breathing her name as still his own!

Joy to the faithful three renewed,
As their glad errand they pursued!
Happy, who so Christ's word convey,
That he may meet them on their way!

So is it still to holy tears,
In lonely hours, Christ risen appears;
In social hours who Christ would see,
Must turn all tasks to Charity.

THE SUN OF RIGHTEOUSNESS.

"We have passed from death unto life."—I. JOHN, iii, 14.

IT is this change in this passage for which the Festival of to-day rejoices. The bondage of the tomb is broken, yes, and a thousand other chains as heavy. There are other prisons thrown open at a Master's touch. A thousand fountains flow at the stroke of his rod. And for all this the world rejoices.

What the change is, which his word and life bring on men, does not appear till we trace it in some contrast, comparing the two careers, that of a man who chooses to drink Immmortality at the Fountain of Life, against him who only looks at the fountain as it runs, plays a minute, perhaps, with the bubbles, and then marches on across a desert with the supplies in his own water-bottles, satisfied with his own provision for the day. They paint pictures sometimes, where the composition shows a palace of luxury on one side and a hovel of misery on the other. The painter tries to contrast the loveliness of skillful gardening against the tangle of the sluggard's desert which jackals and foxes have devoured. But the contrast is worse than that, more sharp and pathetic, between the life, were it only of a twelve-month, of the man who at some season of determination chose Life, which decreed to be called Life, chose Life infinite, or as the Bible says, "Life abundant," or "Life eternal," against the other man who chose Life merely for its good dinners and suppers, for its much money, or perhaps its fine clothes: of the man whose resolves did not have in them the determination to deserve the girl he loved, or to rise to the knowledge he honored, or to serve the world in which he lived. I have pleased myself sometimes, by ‑ imagining the scene and meeting at the Lake of Galilee, say fifteen years after the crucifixion, when Simon Peter and John son of Zebedee might meet there often by apostolic wanderings. There is a good theme for a story, and I will give the hint to any of my friends of the Ladies' Commission or the Sunday School, who would like to adventure in that line of narrative. Let these two apostles meet there some fisherman of their own age, whose name never found itself in any gospel, has never been repeated for the honor of a cathedral, has never been prized and remembered by the founders of a city: some Obed or Micaiah or Nebat, who when in the beginning, the Master of Life came down the lake and said, "Follow me," had listened and determined that he would not follow. If these fools, Andrew and Simon, John and James, and Philip and the rest, the best fishermen on the shore, if they chose to go off and leave their business, so much the worse for them, and so much the better for him. He will supply their customers, and will step into their shoes. He did start at the Master's eagerness. He listened, and then went back to his fishing! Such a man, day after day, would justify to himself his own refusal and would be sure at last that he had done the right thing. Peter and Andrew, James and John had left their boats and had done what the Master bade them. Here were the boats left on the lake; here was all their share in the neglected business. How easily a man who had been hard enough to resist the words of Christ would persuade himself that that was a godsend which relieved him of such rivals. He would now build up a large trade with the garrison at Tiberias, having quite the monopoly of the supply of the port. But he must work quick, for the enthusiasts will be back again.

No! the enthusiasts do not come back. Year by year passes and they do not come back for more than a passing visit. And he, every day, in these years, makes his trip, makes his catch, opens and cleans his fish, goes to the garrison quartermaster with those that suit the Roman taste, and then peddles out what are left here at home to the villagers.

At some one of these passing visits of John the beloved, and of Peter, who used to be such a leader in the little fleet of boats, some neighbor makes a party for them and the three old comrades meet together. It is fifteen years since they parted. Peter is not so arbitrary as he was, and he does not look a day older than he did. He is friendly, cheerful, and tries to recall old times. John does look older. Why he was nothing but a boy when they went away. He is perhaps more reserved now, but still we cannot say "reserved" of a person so sympathetic, who has so much to tell of all sorts of men, and enters so heartily into the secrets of every life.

Imagine the Christian courtesy and readiness with which the two apostles recall the past with their old companion. How they promise to try the boat with him in the morning and see if their hands have lost their old skill. How they tell him of their adventures by sea and land in other parts of the world and of men's customs there. But you will have to imagine at the same time the contrast, as between night and day, between the probable range of his mind, his interests, nay, his loves and his hope, and theirs. They are partners in the Universe, and fellow-laborers with God. He is the owner of one or two boats, and trades with Tiberias in fish. They have enlarged life so much since those early days, that it is like coming back to another world, to come to it. But Life cramps him now more than it did then, for the habits of boyhood and youth unchanged are the habits of a man, and so where the man would have grown, he is only pinched and thwarted by this hard armor.

Such men as John and Peter will not let the visit pass, without using some time, in the sail on the lake, in the talk at the table, to lift this man above thoughts of the salt market and the fish market, the best way to make a corner here, or to secure profit there. And they will succeed. But every time it is they who lift, and he who is lifted. Their Life is real Life, the largest, the loftiest and the deepest. His life, when they find him is it life? is mechanical, small, low and dead, because he has been selfish. And the one token that his nature is like theirs, and his possibilities like theirs, is that he knows that this is so.

It would be easy to imagine just such a contrast between Paul and some old Pharisee companion, as they should meet twenty years after he heard the call of Christ, and waked at Damascus to a life large and true. I wish one of the masters of imagination in such themes, such a man as Charles Kingsley, or William Ware, would work that out for us. It would be a very true romance, and very pathetic. Paul at Jerusalem, just before the Jew mob gathered round him, might, did, I suppose, meet more than one such old fellow-student, class-mate of the old college days of Gamaliel. Paul was prince of gentlemen, and he would have greeted such a man in the most cordial way. Fresh from travel, used to the best society, he had been with scholars, with rulers, prefects and their courts, had seen the leading men of the Hebrew faith all through Greece and Asia Minor, and was in nowise cut off as yet from Jewish communion. And the other for twenty years tithing mint and anise and cumin, at the most arranging a new procession, or intriguing for the election of a high-priest. Paul's range of interests is in nothing less than the establishment absolutely of the Kingdom of God. If you come at his heart of hearts, if he would talk of what in solitude he dreamed of, he would tell you how he saw Cæsar's throne tottering; every altar in the world grown cool; every slave set free, and every chain broken. Nay, this is little. He looks across the veil, as those who see what is invisible. That other world, as men call it, is this world to Paul. That future life, as men say, is now to him. He meets the little country scribe, his old schoolmate, as a Christian gentleman meets a gentleman. But, as when the three parted fishermen met, John and Peter and their friend, so here Paul has to lift, and the other to be lifted. Paul has to lead and the other to be led; for Paul is alive, and the other is dead in his jots and tittles, his forms, rubrics, traditions and commentaries. Paul has entered upon the real life of a child of God. The other is still hammering among things, living as beasts live, and no wonder if he fears to die as they die.

For here is no contrast, observe, between the man who has travelled and him who has staid at home. It is not the contrast between him who has preached to Greeks and Colossians and Ephesians, and him who has served his generation in the walks just as noble of home life. It is not the contrast between the well-informed man and the ill-informed man. No; you find the same contrast in the same house, between two people, neither of whom have left the same town. If you would go with me into some one of these great clusters of houses, where under one roof are contrasts of life as broad as between Greenland and India, I could show you this same contrast there. At one door there should welcome us an old man, the mere beauty of whose face would attract you as you stood at the door. The courtesy of his manner would teach you what is meant by the words, "nature's gentlemen." If it were only in the cheerfulness of his talk, he would lift us above any commonplace or petty range of conversation. Before we knew it, we should be asking him some question, which might perhaps give us the clue to the evenness, grace, bearing and contentment, of an old age so well ordered, of life so well balanced. Yet I cannot vouch for his grammar, and his learning goes scarcely beyond the Bible. While his neighbor—if we are bold enough to make him a visit—has nothing to tell us, and seems to have everything to ask. He has everything to complain of, and he keeps all the interview upon himself. His conflict with things seems to have made him a thing as well. We are glad to escape from the interview, and are at a loss to know how this man is to be lifted any higher than the level which he seems to have chosen. Now the one of these men, as far as one sees, has travelled as much as the other. The one has learned the same external facts as the other. The difference came into their lives, whenever one consciously looked up to God and tried to serve him, and the other consciously looked down and tried to forget him. In those moments one chose unending and unbounded relations for his life, and the other chose dungeons, fetters and all restraints for his. If they both stay at home for ten years, one lives outside himself, ranges in thought and hope through the very streets of the eternal city, meets in companionship with the whole army of prophets and heroes, who have given themselves to the infinite service of mankind. And the other, though they travel sea and land, carries everywhere with him his own hamper; feels everywhere his own pulse, is cursed everywhere with his own heart-aches, and, of necessity, leads but a very petty life, because his life is centred in himself. One of the two is of that class of whom it is said that " you find everywhere a cheerful outlook, a perfect determination to relieve suffering and a certainty that it could be relieved, a sort of sweetness of disposition, which comes from the habit of looking across the line as if death were little or nothing, and with that a disposition to be social, to meet people more than half way." And this is only to say in more words, that this man, the day he became partner in the universe, took all the largeness and accepted all the responsibilities, of Faith, of Hope and Love. But the other trusted nothing, hoped for nothing and loved nobody. For himself he tried to live, and even in that trial failed. For life which deserves the name of life is not possible on these conditions. He vegetated, if it is not disrespect to the vegetables to say so. He existed;

but as you saw, when you met him, he had no life to add to your life, no word to make you cheerful, no experience which you would not fling from you like a burning coal. Unless you could bring him some help there was no reason why you two should come together.

Half the world rouses itself to-day to do honor in some form, simple or elaborate, to that Master of Life, who from such death of selfish separation rouses men to such largeness and reality of a common life. It is as the sun in the heavens, as the spring days lengthen, wakens in every meadow a million blades of grass which he found sleeping. He calls them out of the earth, into a higher life. He quickens them, he fosters them, he attracts them, he compels them so that they draw in the nobler forms of dress, of houses, of light and of heat; and in their little way they too give out of their own power, they breathe out a blessing in their turn. The air is the purer, the perfume is the sweeter because these millions of blades of grass have started out of the cold death of the winter, into the generous mutual life of the new-born year. What the sun in the sky does to those blades of grass, this Sun of Righteousness who is Lord of this Easter Day has done to a million million lives whom he has called from that dead selfishness of lonely and separated life, into communion with each other, into certainty of their own future, into life in common with an infinite God. In that call he takes the name, "Sun of Righteousness." In that name this Sun-Day, day of Light and Heat and Life, becomes his day, or the Lord's Day. Where he speaks and where the child of God listens, listens as Peter and Paul listened, to answer and to follow, there a world of life opens to the vision of that child of God, a world of activity opens upon the will aroused, worlds upon worlds of future life open before the quickened gaze. Yes! The society and companionship even of the infinite God, Lord of heaven and earth, become the august privilege, too great for stumbling words, of him who was yesterday only a fisherman or publican, or a hair-splitting pedant, if to-day he listen to this call. In the wonder-work of the Bible, as Dr. Martineau has said so well, the English peasant is made partaker of the marvels of history and of the world. The Hebrew prophet is in presence of the English tradesman, or domesticated in the Scotch village, is better understood when he speaks of Jordan than even Burns is understood when he celebrates the

Greta, or Wordsworth when he writes of the Yarrow. But this is only one little type or illustration of that free masonry, wider than this world, of him who is partner in the Universe. The Saviour of men looked outside of Galilee, outside this little world, into all worlds, and to all men he offers share in the inheritance and the vision.

But on the other hand, the child of God may refuse to listen. God's child is free, as is his Father. From the word that is spoken he may turn away. Like Satan in the poem, he may turn from his place in the Empire of Heaven, and in some under-world create for himself a kingdom of his own. The blade of grass, which is summoned to-day to throw off the clod above it, must obey. Though it be deep down in the dark earth, the living heat of the sun penetrates,—where the light cannot strike down,—and the germ must start to consciousness, must find its own way up to light and love, must live and grow. But man may resist to the bitter end. To the fisherman at Bethsaida, who stands where Peter stands, the call comes, as it comes to Peter, and the fisherman may say "No," or perhaps he will not care even to speak, but will quietly turn away from Infinite Life, and with his eyes open, choose to-day's chance at fishing as better. When Saul hears the plaintive call, "Saul, Saul, why dost thou persecute me?." there is some other dabster over forms, whose name is all forgotten, who hears a like cry, plaintive and tender, and shuts his ears, as if he did not hear. And so to-day, among these thousand tokens of life renewed, among a thousand glories of life, among all the tokens and treasures of infinite beauty, infinite wisdom, infinite love, it is possible still to refuse to commune with God, to refuse to look into heaven, to refuse to share and share with these companions. Such prerogative of freedom man enjoys. He can close his eyes, he can close his ears, he can harden his heart, he can live—men do live—as the beasts live, so that he shall die—men do die —with as little hope and joy as the beasts die withal. But our Easter morning wakes us, with its storm of perfume, music, love, light and glory, that we may tread under our feet such fetters of bondage. With all its voices and all its memories it allures us that we may pass from death unto life, in the new birth of a higher being, of those WHO LIVE IN LOVE.

THE FAREWELL AT AZAN.

BY EDWIN ARNOLD.

FAREWELL, friends! Yet not farewell;
Where I am, ye, too, shall dwell.
I am gone before your face,
A moment's time, a little space.
When ye have come where I have stepped
Ye will wonder why ye wept;
Ye will know, by wise love taught,
That here is all, and there is naught.
Weep awhile, if ye are fain,—
Sunshine still must follow rain;
Only not at death,—for death,
Now I know, is that first breath
Which our souls draw when we enter
Life, which is of all life centre.

Be ye certain all seems love,
Viewed from Allah's throne above;
Be ye stout of heart, and come
Bravely onward to your home!
La 'Allah illa Allah! yea!
Thou love divine! Thou love alway!

He that died at Azan gave
This to those who made his grave.

THE LIFE WAS THE LIGHT OF MEN.

Our Southern Indians worshipped the Rising Sun. The chief of the Natchez tribe, who was its priest, mounted early upon the high hill which they had perhaps made for such worship, and with the first ray of the glad light made signal to the waiting throng that the new day's life had come. Their morning worship is the announcement of their daily joy that light gives life, and that light and life are one.

That savage worship suggests the eager purport of this text of St. John. He is using the fanciful language of the fooleries of his time, for better purpose than it has ever borne before. He would fain, if he can, make those who read, remember that the world has its light as it has its life from the one God who makes it and orders it. It does not, as the Egyptian doctrine of Æons implied, receive Light from one source and Life from another, it does not go here for its Truth and there for its Love. The gifts of God are not thus divided in various arsenals, nor are we treated as some wretched commander is treated, who has to send to one department for his powder, to another for his shot, to another for his shells, sent to Washington for his instructions, and to Alaska for his men. The Life of the world is the Light of the world, and its Light is its Life. "We have all received of his Fullness," indeed, as he takes care soon to say, and as James says, in his Epistle, we all, when we choose, "partake of the Divine nature."

The world's theologians, in its recent days, have been generally men who learned what little they knew from books, from such oracles as nominative cases and verbs, and have learned them with the errors that to such limited methods belong. It is not unnatural then that their habit of speaking of the Saviour of men should have become a habit of making him such a one as themselves. Their Christ is one who has a doctrine to teach. He has obtained information which he is to impart. We are to go to him for Light, and we are to carry this Light to others. What he brings to us is a Revelation. All this indeed is true, nor can there be any possible harm in compelling the world to receive it. But then, why here is only a very little of the truth! How is it that this Christ teaches me the Golden Rule? How is it that he compels me to pray in the Lord's Prayer? How is it that when I hear the parable of the Prodigal Son, I know that God and man are united in the union there described? It is because here is the Life of Men. It is because the Life of the World grows, thrives, enjoys, succeeds, lives, when the World takes in and takes on this habit of Life. When the World is one with its God as he is, then the World knows what it is to Live.

It is perfectly true, as persons indifferent to Christianity point out, that Jesus Christ did not first discover, reveal, or point out the Immortality of man. No indeed! In that matter, as in all others, "God had never left himself without a witness." Martha had stammered out at her brother's grave, "I know that he shall rise again at the Last Day." Plenty of announcements before of man's immortality. But the marvel of the Saviour's work, and the Miracle of Easter, is that he makes men believe these announcements, and take them into the field and purport of their daily Life. As he himself says, he not only comes that men may have Life, but he comes that they may have it more abundantly than they had it before. He makes them Live with Life so true, and their Life is so large and full, that they know that it does not end with the physical accident of death. With every hour of such Life, men feel better the great words, "*I Am*," with which God describes his always present being. Or, if we speak of texts, such men know better the meaning of the Saviour's own words when he says, so simply, "Because I live, ye shall live also."

Our business on Easter morning is to compare the large life of the world, as he set it throbbing, enjoying, enlarging and truly living, with what the world called life when he was born into it. It is this contrast between life dying, gasping and almost dead, and the life of to-day, exulting, triumphing and increasing, which justifies our Easter rejoicings. Compare, for instance, the life of a child, as Jesus found childhood, against the life of a child as it exists in all Christian lands to-day. When Herod the Great, with one stroke, killed all the children in Bethlehem, he did nothing which was much out of the way, in his own habit, or indeed, in the history of his time. He killed so many of his own children indeed, that in a joke, long remembered, the Emperor said he had rather be Herod's hog, than Herod's son. When he killed the children in Bethlehem, nobody could say him nay, but I suppose in strictness, he then only used the power of the strongest. But when he killed his own children, he was wholly within his own rights, at Roman law. Children were nothing, they had no rights, one might say they had no lives of their own, until there came this infinite enlargement of life in which we live. We call it Christianity. In this life the new-born infant, also, is recognized as a child of God, born into the family and partner in its privileges and its duties. You may see the old system now in any untamed savage tribe. If the march is too long or too hard for the boy or girl, if boy or girl winces under the burden which is divided between them and the dogs, the blow of a hatchet leaves the child's body on the trail, and the march goes on unencumbered.

It is from such daily death that the child who was born in Bethlehem lifts all childhood into a larger life.

And so also of the life of women. In Palestine, undoubtedly it was at its very best. Nothing in Greek or Roman or Egyptian life, in that day, compares for freedom or for largeness, with such a life as Mary Mother could have led in Nazareth, or any other peasant woman of Galilee. But Palestine is only a speck on the world's surface, and though you bring to bear on literature all the light you can, though you may read between the lines as boldly as you dare, you only find that the women of the time, the best and noblest of them are straws upon the current of the world's life. They are sometimes the playthings of sovereigns, they sometimes rise to the dignity of ornaments, and sometimes a Cleopatra leads an Antony to his ruin. But that woman like man is living and moving in the infinite work and purpose of God, that she may light new lights in the world's darkness, and plant new seed in its deserts, that woman with man is put into the world to subdue it, that God entrusts to her as to him the making it a part of his heaven, this appears nowhere in literature or in history, till the Marys and Salomes take their share in the life of the Gospels, until Mary Magdalene teaches Simon Peter his great lesson at an open tomb. If one could say nothing more, one would be forced to say this, that the working power of the world was at least doubled when the new life thus entrusted to woman her half of the work which God entrusts to all his children.

In another way, and by other lines, the new life which dates from this day creates all modern commerce, all modern discovery and invention, almost all modern manufactures even, and agriculture; certainly all modern science, modern law, modern government, and so modern civilization. The world has been perfectly right in drawing the line at Easter morning which separates its ancient history from its modern history, its old from its new. Thursday night, Jesus Christ himself might call the ideal Satan "the Prince of this world." "The Prince of this world cometh, and hath nothing in me." But let Good Friday pass, and let Easter morning come, and from Easter morning for nineteen hundred years, or for nineteen thousand, Jesus Christ is Prince of this world, King of Kings, and Lord of Lords. At his word, as I say, modern commerce starts into being. That little catechism I read here last Sunday, "The Teaching of the Twelve Apostles," teaches his law of life to a few stragglers in Greece. "This is the way to live," it says. "Thou shalt love the Lord thy God, and thou shalt love thy neighbor as thyself." "What a poor crumb is that," you say, to throw out upon the dark, wild waters of an angry world. Crumb if you please, but this I know, that in the fullness of time, if a tradesman on one side the world choose to write to the tradesmen the other side of the world this letter, "Send me twenty ships laden with your wheat, and I will send you whatever you bid me in recompense." I know that that request will be honored. It shall be flashed through the ocean in an instant, in less time than it takes Juno to send from one side Mt. Olympus to another. And without an instant's hesitation, it will be honored by a man who never saw the sender and never will see him, who is of another nation, another language, and another law. This will come about, and in less than nineteen hundred years, because all men are brethren and at bottom know they are brethren, because they mean to bear one another's burdens. That is to say, the mutual confidence, which is centre and secret of all modern commerce, is really born from the new life. "I, if I be lifted up, will bring all men unto me."

Work out for yourself if you can, the contrasted picture of the commerce of that day. Imagine the lordly purveyor for the tables of Tiberius. There comes to him one morning, as he sits in his cabinet, a favorite of the Emperor. "Marcus," he says, "our lord has heard from a great traveller of a new luxury. At the other end of Asia they use a tonic drink which cheers them, as wine does not cheer us, and yet it does not intoxicate. They use it as a dried leaf, which they steep in boiling water. Our lord bids you provide it, and tell me, when can it be here?" The purveyor replies in dismay, " I also had heard of this elixir, but I had hoped no tidings of it would ever come to our Master's ears. Say to him that in three years from this day, if the lives of my messengers are spared, he shall taste the infusion at the festival of Bacchus." And then in his dejection, he calls his most successful traveller, he gives him two or three diamonds to stitch into his girdle, he gives him what would buy a hundred slaves for his expenses of travel. He is to go to the farthest East, and to return with as much of this new elixir as he can safely bear upon his person. And he must be in Rome again before three years have gone by. But, long before that time, alas! his diamonds have been blazing in the crests of Kurdish princes and his bones have been whitening in the Kurdish desert. And when the feast of Bacchus comes, the Emperor of half the world must celebrate it without the new sensation.

It would be worth while to trace out the same contrast in the difference between agriculture, manufactures, navigation, literature, art and science, now and then. There is hardly a single detail, where the contrast is not as strong as that between a man fumbling at midnight for a tool which he cannot find, and the same man working with the same tool in the clear sunlight of noon-day. And in each of these contrasts, we should find what must serve us as one example in detail of the world's resurrection from the dead to-day ; it is the way in which the new life of the world calls The People into being. Whole nations, alas! have not yet heard this call. Many of what are called Christian kingdoms do not understand it. Even the great democratic governments like ours, falter and are afraid of it. But all the same it sounds steadily and makes itself intelligible. " God has made of one blood all nations of the world," and, " He who is greatest among you shall be your minister." These are the central lights for the guidance of this New Departure. Little wonder that the common people always heard him gladly, the carpenter of Nazareth. Little wonder that priests and rulers heard him with terror and suspicion. It was so in the beginning, it will be so to the end. But more and more the truth shines out, that every baby born into the world is child of God, infinite and eternal. Every such child must be entrusted with every privilege, must be trained with every care. For every such child is born to these infinite possibilities. Give to the child full chance, the chance which you would give to an imagined archangel, and there is no saying to what that possibility shall come. Trust to the full, God's abundant love and give to each child the best you know how to give, for its health, its happiness, its growth, and its education, or in one word for its life, and then you gain infinite power though you were in a New England township or a Swiss canton. It is power for invention, power for discovery, power for research, power for teaching and for learning, power for enlarging the world's life in short, such as no Tiberius in Capri, no Crœsus in Sardis ever dreamed of, and such as their wealth and power could never command. For a hundred and fifty years, while in a half feudal system, your American colonies maintain one class of proprietaries, one class of gentlemen, one class of laborers, and one class of slaves, while to one and another they dole out rights and privileges with unequal hand, according as the baby is born in a log-cabin or in a house of cedar, so long things stand still for America. But once destroy this paper system, as Copernicus destroyed the imagined mechanism of Ptolemy, once speak to all your people, poor and rich, black and white, fools and learned in a Saviour's words, once say, and mean it when you say it, "One is your Father, and all ye are brethren." Say this as if you meant it, and not with the decorous mouthing of the pulpit or of a liturgy. Say to all priests and all noblemen that you mean it, and to all laborers and all slaves that you mean it. Let your laws echo it. Make your constitutions as if this and only this were true. Then even a palsied land will take up its bed and walk. Here in America, so soon as that word was spoken, though the laughing critics call it a "gilded generality," there was no wilderness where man's foot did not enter, there was no ocean he did not traverse, no mountain which he did not cut down, and no valley which was not exalted. Man is told he is child of God. He tries the experiment. And lo! what they told him is so. He too rides on the whirlwind and controls the storm. Born in a hovel, if you please. Yes! but he becomes the greatest of his brethren for all that, if only he accept the Gospel rule, and live in the Gospel life, if only he make himself the servant of all.

It is not in these beautiful flowers only, it is not in the Easter eggs only, in the opening crocus, in the song of our robins, or in the baptism of our darling children, that we are to find the symbols of Easter, or its trophies. There is not one comfort or joy of our modern life which would be in any sort possible to us, but for the larger life which, in Jesus Christ, the world began to live in his life and gospel. So true is it, that his gospel is not a lesson simply, but a life. It is the Light of the world, but that is because it is the Life of the world. You know I am fond of saying that these little children of ours are born into the Christian Church. They are of it, beyond peradventure. It was a Christian blanket which warmed the baby's naked limbs. It was Christian science that saved the baby's life. It was the Christian coal burned in a Christian furnace which warmed the Christian home in which the Christian child lived, where the child of the savage would have died, had the wretched wife of the savage tarried in such a winter to give him life. But each one of us may learn the same lesson in his own home. The food upon the table, the flowers from the greenhouse, the morning newspaper, the street car in which I rode to church, the casting of the bell which sounded in the tower, the tones of the organ which spoke to me of peace and triumph in its harmonies, the inspiration of the music of the Easter anthem, nay! even the cunning of the hand which designed the font for baptism are only offshoots of the Life of the world, which lives, because Jesus Christ lived and died and rose again.

"Because I live, ye shall live also."

"The things that I do, ye shall do also, and greater things than these shall ye do."

"For I, if I be lifted up, will draw all men unto me."

"In Him was Life, and the Life was the Light of Men."

THE SECRET PLACE OF THE MOST HIGH.

BY WILLIAM C. GANNETT.

The Lord is in His Holy Place
   In all things near and far,
Shekinah of the snow flake, He,
   And glory of the star,
And Secret of the April-land
   That stirs the field to flowers,
Whose little tabernacles rise
   To hold Him through the hours.

He hides Himself within the love
   Of those that we love best;
The smiles and tones that make our homes
   Are shrines by Him possessed.
He tents within the lonely heart
   And shepherds every thought.
We find Him not by seeking long,
   We lose Him not unsought.

So though we build a Holy Place
   To be our Sinai-stand,
The Holiest of Holies still
   Is never made by hand.
Our Sinai needs the listening ear,
   Our Garden needs the vow:
"Thy will be done,"—and lo! Thy voice,
   Thy vision as we bow!

IMMORTAL.

"What is mortal may be swallowed up of life."—2 CORINTHIANS, v, 4.

"It is a little thing in comparison to believe in immortality. The great thing is to live as an immortal." This fundamental statement, made nearly in these words by Rev. John Weiss, a man of rare religious genius, announces the central truth, which gives the real value to the festivities of to-day. The joy of the new Life, the jubilee triumph because Life is larger than it once was, and is to be larger than it is, the new strength, the new health, the new certainty which come to the world because its life is larger than it was, all these are quite impossible to beasts who die, as they are impossible to clocks which stop when the weights have run down. They all belong to the victories of Immortal beings, who know they are Immortal.

And the lesson of Easter for you and me, we would seek a lesson, will be learned, if we rightly ask what eternal beings do, who have such senses, such muscles, such hopes and fears as we, and if we find an answer. What is there which a man can achieve, looking forward and able to look forward, which a brute cannot achieve, because he does not look forward and cannot? How does this surety of eternity affect daily life, what I say, what I plan, and what I do? I read a speech of Julius Cæsar and he tells me, that when a blood vessel breaks, my life stops forever. But I do not believe that my life stops forever, because that mere button in my dress gives way. How will that difference between me and Cæsar affect what I think and say and do?

Mr. Ruskin lays it down as a canon of art, that no painting should ever shut us up in an interior, so completely, but that the eye may somewhere struggle beyond, and see through a window, through a doorway, through a passage between columns or a rift in the trees, to the infinite blue of an infinite heaven. Whoever has to change the composition of his picture, so as to do this, to change from the mere sketch of a room shut up, to that larger scheme, which includes that bit of heaven, knows very well that the change is no simple change of one or two details. Every color must be changed, every light and every shadow. Our relations now are with infinite affairs, and the infinite considerations which we have brought in, will affect everything with which we have to do. The mere camera, indeed, which I have focused for an object the other side of the room, needs entire re-adjustment, before I direct it to an object the other side the river or the bay. And that single hint as to a different perspective for near drawing, or distant, carries us far. The little child has to learn to see. First of all she sees her own hands and learns to know that these fingers are her own. It is a step, a happy step, when beyond the hands and outside of them, she learns the face of her mother, always ready, always kind, almost always near, but alas, sometimes away! But the whole machinery of vision must be changed, and the whole process of thought enlarged, when the infant knowledge which perceives and comprehends these two, goes farther, and knows the curtain and the window, and, at last, the rattle or the straw. It is by successive steps from these that the child at last conceives the idea of distance, which is not natural indeed to an infinite soul, and learns how to measure in a fashion the difference between the tree in the garden, and the chair in the room. Here is, on a small scale, and with steps which are petty in comparison, the process of the enlargement of vision alone. With that enlargement comes the growth and enlargement of every other faculty, nay! the growth of mind itself which controls such faculties, and in the end the enlargement of that soul which commands the mind to come and go about its business. It is in that enlargement, as this text puts it, that the mortal is clothed upon with the immortal. A mortal man now begins to live and move and think and speak as an immortal being does.

In Mrs. Trimmer's story of "The Robins," a child's book, now forgotten in the nursery, the brightest sentence was the exclamation of one of the half-fledged little birds, who, having flown out of the nest for the first time, cries out to its mother, "What a very large place the world is." When the little robin is fully fledged, she will be able to fly above the apple tree, and will see that the orchard, which was but just now so large a world, fills in truth a space very small in a world which has become much bigger. And if the robin could soar like the lark, the circle of the horizon would expand again, the hills but just now distant would in their turn become near, and with a very different sense, she would be crying again, "How very large is the world!" And yet this horizon is nothing if robin or lark learn to look into the sun, like the eagle, or if, by this time, there come the unanswerable question, "What is there beyond the sun?" or, "What is there beyond the farthest star?"

All these enlargements of the horizon are little analogies of what happened to the literature of the world, when the new world was born and the old world ended. That is to say, when literature began to speak of man as being an immortal instead of talking of him as a mere brute, with the gift of speech, who, at the best, stopped living at three score, or say four score years. Compare the book of Proverbs, for instance, with Paul's Letter to the Philippians. The first is as wise as you please. It is very bright. It is useful. It is practical. It is shrewd. It is even humorous in places. But then! it is all so narrow, so restricted! You turn over to the end to look for something more. Is it possible, you say, that this is all these men had to say about life, when they were so sharp and keen? Why! this is not life, they talk about, this is nothing but clockwork, the swing of the pendulum here, and the twitch of the second hand there. From this you turn over to the Epistle to the Philippians. It is all jubilant with the joy and confidence of divine being! You are not saying anything about heaven perhaps, but you talk like a person who is in heaven. He who writes really knows what the joy of God is, the joy of creating, the joy of sustaining, the joy of living and loving forever. That is the reason why this exile, writing in a prison to a handful of provincials, the most prosperous of whom was peddling dye-stuffs for a living, keeps saying, "Rejoice evermore! Rejoice in the Lord. The Lord is at hand." And Paul speaks with that large certainty which has in the end preserved this little letter of his so that it is remembered everywhere among the classics of good cheer and enthusiasm. It speaks the pass-words and rallying cries. "Forgetting the things which are behind and stretching forward to the things which are before."

On the whole, this is the contrast between the Old Testament and the New Testament, though in the great, glad exceptions the Old Testament is prophetic. Still, speaking in general, what harasses you as you read your book of Kings or of Chronicles, is the feeling, perhaps undefined, that this all belongs to a corner of Asia, and perhaps to the life of some Gideon or Barak, of whom you know little and perhaps care less. In the New Testament, you are on different ground, and are breathing a different atmosphere. And when you look for the horizon to your picture, there is none. These men who write and talk, speak as immortals to an immortal; and, for the instant, you cannot but accept their postulate. In their company you are as one of them. And he, the leader of them all, who starts them on this line of address, at once so simple and so large, he takes from first to last the ground that as he is Son of God you are God's sons and daughters, that you share the infinite life. Death? What is it? They who truly live can never die.

And you might make the same contrast between classical literature and all modern literature. Man is a much larger being to the writer of our time than he was to Virgil or Livy or Herodotus, and it is this truth which asserts itself whether there be any formal allusion to his immortality or no. Indeed, since what we call modern history comes in, you may almost measure men against each other by comparing them as an infinite purpose, the purpose of an immortal, comes into their enterprise or does not. Thus Columbus went and came that God, in Jesus Christ, might be the ruler of this world. The wealth of the Indies should redeem the Holy Sepulchre. The people of the Indies should bow before the cross. The world should be one world, and Jesus Christ should be its King. What follows on plans so large, in a range so wide, is that men rate Columbus as one of the first of men and rate him rightly. But if you had asked within twenty years of his death who was the first man of his time you would not have heard his name. Men would have talked to you of that Emperor who was enrolling navies and compelling armies. But alas! the Emperor had no object but himself, and to-day he is only another Goliath or Ajax, a savage on a throne wearing a crown, without any of the purposes of immortality. Such a man dies, and in a generation, in less than a generation, there is nobody left to pretend he is first of men.

And let any man to-day take for leading motives the motives which might impel Uriel or Abdiel, or any other servant of God who is not worried by fear of death, or of what may follow it. Let a man live with God, not afraid to talk with him. Let him study God's plans and methods, as one of Michael Angelo's pupils might study his. Let him work in nature's laboratory, tracing the present processes of creation as they go on to-day when the lily opens, or let him study history, and in the evolution of century from century see what it is which is weak, and what that is which prevails, how vice and crime are powerless and bring forth no issue, and how righteousness exalts a nation. Or let a man undertake, with other men and women, what he might suppose an angel would do, not fettered by time nor anxious about its passage. Let him range from hovel to garret in seeking his society, let him house with crime if he can so help crime, let him carry comfort to beggary, and teach beggary the secrets of industry. Let him live with men for men, not as if the clothes that he wears, or the viands he eats were of the first import. Such life with God is what the Saints mean by Faith. Such life for men is what they mean by Love. The man who bids his life move in such causes, starts to-day on the career of an immortal. His mortal house is clothed upon with his house which is from heaven. He lives as an immortal lives. He opens a window into the infinite, through this dead, blank wall which did shut off his prospect. He changes the focus of his camera, and his foreground is no longer distorted and twisted. And, while he does this, he finds that that third element of an immortal's life takes on certainty. What Paul calls Hope, by which he means living in the future while a man lives in to-day, is all the time growing stronger and more a thing of course were it only by exercise. He uses what he has, and because he uses it, he has more.

I was talking to a near friend of the English General Gordon since he died, and in a downcast way, which I will confess was time-born and time-bred, I said sadly enough, that it seemed a pity that such a life as that, so devoted to the noblest purpose, should be cut short almost at the moment of success, because a lying Arab stole in behind him, and smote him to his death, when he could not defend himself. His friend had caught so much of his spirit, that he turned on me almost as if I had spoken blasphemy. "Oh, no!" he cried, "he would never have said that himself. Why, he was for himself eager for the larger life.

And you could have pleased him no more than to show to him that it was coming soon. And see to-day," he added, " how much more power he has over men, to lead them as he will, than he had only a year ago!" This does not mean, as Paul says so wisely, that Gordon sought to be unclothed. He had no wish to throw his life away. No, it is the wish " to be clothed upon ; " to have one's earthly life and work so built upon, so glorified and aggrandized by the large powers of an infinite existence, that one may subdue the things of life,—food, clothing, luxury, money, houses, land and the rest,—and keep them under entirely. So one shall command principalities and powers, things present and to come. " Ye shall tread on serpents and scorpions, and nothing shall by any means hurt you."

To think of to-day's work as a part of the infinite work, to speak even of to-day's affair as belonging in the service one is to render twenty centuries hence, this is an immortal's habit. An early friend of mine, whom I tried to describe under the name of Harry Wadsworth, and whom some of you young people know by that name, had this habit so completely that I find old friends of his speaking of him, as if that were perhaps the characteristic by which most often they remembered him. As a man who has lived in China and is going to live there again, unconsciously speaks with a different measurement of Suffolk county and of Boston, though he never allude to a detail in that other home of his, so such men impress you as having lived in heaven and meaning to live there again. And here the comparison fails us. For the reason why such men and women give this impression, is that they live in heaven now. For as a man may be a son of Massachusetts, and at the same time be a loyal citizen of the United States, yes, and may give to the National Administration the larger part of his thought and care, almost forgetting that there are Massachusetts politics or administration ; so a man on this earth may be so interested in Faith and Hope and Love, which are the infinite elements of Eternal being, that what is merely earthly, eating and drinking and sleeping, shall be quite subordinate. And this double life, shall I call it? is what Paul means, when he says the life on earth is clothed upon with our life which is from heaven.

And if it so happen to any of us, that, in the course of promotion from world to world, one of our very nearest friends, whose life is all knit into our life, is called from service here to higher service there, then we are called to a communion with heaven, whether we would or no, and at least in the thought of him who has gone before us, we are living as immortals live. Mrs. Stowe has well said of the death of children, that there is hardly one household, where the gulf between this world and the other world has not been bridged over when such a child, so dear, so sure to be remembered, passed from shore to shore. "Where my treasure is, my heart is." And, as one after another leave me here, I am the more apt, whether I meant it or no, to cross over, were it only in my questionings and imaginations, to ask them questions, or to ask God questions about them, and I am the more apt, in the twilight, to sit and wait for the help that they have asked from God for me, and which is sure to come. Because they have left me, I am the more sure to live the life of Faith, of Hope, and of Love.

Easter morning does not prove man's immortality. It asserts it. In the universal resurrection from the night of winter, as Life returns which has been sleeping or shrouded, it asserts man's communion and companionship with the God who is life : and it declares that man, who is child of God, cannot die. Because he is immortal he can adjust his life with the Infinite Perspective. Because he is immortal, he can come to his God as an immortal comes, can speak, can listen and can reply again. Because he is immortal, he arranges his duties on the scale of immortality. He begins if he chooses, on what shall task him a thousand years to finish : he enters on this enterprise or that, perfectly sure that he has infinite allies. Is one of these allies called away so that he does not see his face? It is as a fellow officer might be sent on other service in the campaign, whom he is to meet again in the hour of victory. Because he is immortal, he lives with these and for these who also are immortal. They have perhaps help for him, he has perhaps help for them. Help or not, each has for each, companionship, and it is not to be that they are to grind along through ages of ages, stupid and alone.

To renew such immortal life here, of Faith and Hope and Love, is the mission every year of Easter Day. That this which is mortal may be clothed upon with immortality.

LISTENING.

BY W. C. GANNETT.

I hear it often in the dark,
   I hear it in the light,—
Where is the voice that calls to me
   With such a quiet might?
It seems but echo to my thought
   And yet beyond the stars;
It seems a heart-beat in a hush,
   And yet the planet jars!

Oh, may it be that far within
   My inmost soul there lies
A *spirit-sky* that opens with
   Those voices of surprise?
And can it be, by night and day,
   That firmament serene
Is just the heaven where God himself,
   The Father, dwells unseen?

O God within, so close to me
   That every thought is plain,
Be judge, be friend, be Father still
   And in Thy heaven reign!
My heaven is mine, my very soul,
   Thy words are sweet and strong,
They fill my inward silences
   With Music and with Song.

They send me challenges to right
   And loud rebuke my ill,
They ring my bells of victory,
   They breathe my "Peace, be still!"
They ever seem to say, "My child,
   Why seek Me so all day?
Now journey inward to thyself
   And listen by the way."

MANY HOMES.

"In my Father's house are many mansions. If it were not so, I would have told you; for I go to prepare a place for you."—JOHN xiv, 2.

As the declaration in which the Saviour lifted the curtain highest, the text is studied, of course, with curious, even anxious, interest. There is, it seems, a heaven for each of us, whatever his mood or his attainment; and it seems that, as Jesus thought of it, these might be quite different each from each. One thing more, which our stately word "mansion" does not teach, but which appears distinctly in the original text, and in all that Jesus ever says of heaven,—these places which he prepares are so many homes. Your home is ready for you, mine for me. The text would be better rendered, indeed, if we read, "In my Father's house are many homes."

1. Whatever we know, and whatever we believe, of these homes, on the other side of the line, is, as St. Paul says, spiritually known and "spiritually judged." To Jesus Christ, living in the Spirit of God, led by the Spirit,—or, as we say, leading a life wholly spiritual,—the whole sense of these realities, what I may call the sight of them, the hearing and conception of them, was perfectly clear. To us it is clear or not clear, strong or faint, according as our lives are lives of the spirit or of the flesh; according as we live for things that die, or for the three realities which endure.

And here is the answer to the frequent question, why Jesus Christ himself, with his clear vision of the infinite life, gave us no more description of it, nor other pictures of it, than are in these words. What is the use of pictures to a person who cannot see, or of descriptions to one who cannot understand? I could throw upon the wall yonder, from a *camera obscura*, a perfect picture of the Temple of the Parthenon. But while your backs were turned to it you could not see it; nay, even if I begged you to turn round, and you complied, you could not see while the church was all aglow with this light; while you were looking upon each other in this sunlight. The image is there, but it is an image you cannot discern. Only a few of those nearest could just make out some of its leading lines, its highest lights and deepest shades. It would not be till we had screened off all the cross-lights from our own sunshine; till we could no longer see carpet, cushion, chandelier, persons, or anything around, that the picture there would be clear, and sharp, and real. No revealer can reveal anything to us which we have not the spiritual power at least to apprehend, and in a measure to comprehend. If you want pictures of heaven you must go to Mahomet, or to those expounders of Christianity who adopt the fashions of Mahomet. He will give you flowers and gardens to your taste; but even he can do no more than meet the taste he finds. Jesus reserves what he might have said, because unless those who heard him are of spiritual life, habit, and experience, which is to say, unless they are exercised in Faith, Hope, and Love, why, they cannot understand, see, or hear of the spiritual heaven, of a heaven of Faith, Hope, and Love. He did not make, therefore, the fatal error which teachers of children make, who, with a poor earthly fancy, describe to the poor little things that before which the loftiest heavenly imagination is silent,—a mistake which, if it has any fruit, results in binding them for years to a heaven which is only a garden, or only a shop of jewels, or a king's palace, according as the childish allegory may have taught them.

I think that some of those who hear me may remember the "Child's Book of the Soul," the name of which carried it into Sunday-school libraries a generation ago. The amiable and well-meaning author, himself, indeed, a practical philosopher of no mean power, attempted the impossible. He would describe the indescribable. He would define the infinite. So he bade his unfortunate little readers take their school slates, and with short marks of the slate-pencil, crowded as close as possible together, cover, first one side, and then the other. Then he bade them imagine all the children who ever lived in the world, since the world began, using the whole of their lives, through all the period known to history, by marking slates in this manner. Then he bade them fancy that each mark on each slate represented a thousand million years of human existence. And you anticipate the sublime close of the highly elaborated chapter, as it told these little children that all the white marks on all the slates, representing all these congeries of thousands of millions of years, would amount literally to nothing in comparison to the infinite existence of God's children living with him. Of all such elaborate effort, for what the fortunate slang of our time calls "materialization," an English critic said, happily, that the very best you could hope, after the little children had struggled through this chapter, would be that they should always think of heaven as a gigantic slate quarry, in which they should live forever.

And such, in truth, is the result of any human effort, by any human language, to describe that which is in itself, of its very essence, purely spiritual. The description of a spiritual heaven, though it were perfectly wrought out by an archangel, would be as unintelligible to the carnal mind as the heaven itself.

So is it that the only statement of detail which the Saviour gives is this in the text; which translated into our habit of speech, says this,— that whatever be the heaven which we are prepared for when we pass from this world that spiritual life we shall have. Our homes are there such as we ourselves have made them. If your highest joy be the counting out of rubies, or the dressing your person with diamonds, Omnipotence itself will not force you into life more spiritual. There are many mansions there. That is to say, the economy of the life before us is the same as that of life here in its variety, and in its adaptation to each separate soul.

This is the Christian statement of life without these bodies,—of the future life. It differs wholly from the best speculations which it found in the world. As widely does it differ from what I am tempted to call the "half-and-half statements" of to-day. Do we not hear speculations from people who think of God from their knowledge of what men have been? Such a man—if God had let such a man stand by him when human life began—would take for granted, at once, that the world was always to be peopled with myriads of exact duplicates of Adam, all exactly alike, and all mechanically pulsing at the beat of one heart-throb. That seems to be mechanical man's highest notion of the highest victory. A million clocks of the same pattern, of which all the parts are mutually inter-changeable! An army of perfectly drilled soldiers! A factory of consentaneous looms! And so, mechanical man, in his uniform, shoe-last conception, can frame for himself no better notion of heaven than that it is an ocean of God, into which, bit by bit, we melt away. Here we are, blocks of ice, such men tell us, which, in that life, will melt back into the one ocean which shall engulf us all.

But, as you see, the Christian statement is not hampered by any such pettiness of the slate-quarry or of the machine-shop. The God who chooses to make this world a world of unity in variety; a world whose countless forests are made of countless trees, of which the countless leaves are never twice the same; a world of men, each differing from each, and each free; the God whose grandeur is so much greater than our grandeur, whose success is so much more successful than our success, and whose variety is so infinitely beyond our tame uniformity,—this God chooses for his heaven the same infinity of ornament and design. One star of it differs from another star in glory. Each angel life in it differs from each other life. So, for each life, there is a different mansion. "In my Father's house are many homes."

Just as, on earth, the boy and his father, the girl and her mother, the oldest child in a family, the second child and the youngest child; the sick and the well, the old and the young, live in spheres different each from each,—so in all life, life there and here, each shall find himself in his own home, bearing his own character, and living his own life. Because love is one of the three elements of heaven these homes are homes of mutual life. As there is society here so there is there; sympathy here and sympathy there; kindred hearts fuse together here and they fuse together there. But the mansions are different mansions there as here. It is no ghastly caravansary, poorhouse, or palace, where Room 99 is like Room 1, and Room 1000 like Room 99. It is a myriad multitude of Homes. There are many spheres of duty, many voices in chorus. There are different trees to water—if you call it a garden— and different flowers to train, as in the old paradise,—where, when Adam

> "Taught the tangled ivy how to climb,
> Eve, in a wild of roses, intermixed with myrtle,
> Found what to redress till noon."

2. All this is of interest to us, as it gives us help in to-day's calamities, and incentive and life in to-day's duties. Wherever any man is in his spiritual life, just there is heaven ready for him *now*. Just there,

and so does he conceive it; and, for all the purposes of his well-being, he conceives it in the best possible way,—he conceives it rightly. Not, of course, that it is a complete or adequate conception; but it is as much as will do him any good. For all the intents and purposes of his advancement this is his heaven.

Describe heaven for another, and insist on your description,—whether it be a heaven of harps, like Dr. Watts's, or of piano-fortes, like a more modern author's of our own time,—you drive your pupil right away from it, unless he be a precise counterpart of yourself who make the description. An eager student will tell a child that in heaven he shall always learn; and the child, hating book-learning, really dreads such a heaven. An eager spirit, always on the alert, preaches that in heaven there shall be no pause in its activity. Heaven, like earth, is to be eager planning, forward marching, and every success a stepping-stone for new plans and other marches. What a wound is this to the aged heart which has tossed long enough in the gales of life to be longing for a harbor! The best story they tell of Calvin, and one which does something to redeem him in our affections, is the story which tells of his quick insight when some such contriver had been describing heaven to him. This teacher described to him the golden glass which was the floor of heaven, and told him he was to look down through its transparency and enjoy the sight of the sufferings of the damned in the abyss below. The young Calvin was child of God enough to answer in scorn, "I had rather live with the damned below than with the saints above in such a heaven as that is." And we need not go back for such anecdotes three hundred years. I am afraid that many of us can remember the gloom which has fallen upon our exuberant youth, when exuberant youth was taught that heaven was a place of eternal Sunday, or that the saints are to have no occupation there but the perpetual singing of psalms.

Such is the result, and a deserved result, of the best pictures your poor fancy can paint, if you are bigot enough, after the fashion of creed-makers, to try to fix them, and to say this is all just so. For its stimulus, for its faith, for its hope, and for perfect love, the soul wishes to enter not your heaven, but its own. The Saviour knows this when he says, "In my Father's house are many homes."

Do not let me obtrude upon boy or girl in any such bigotry, by telling of my own boyish imaginings. Rather I may help boy or girl if I can make them understand how as one grows in years and in strength, as this world grows larger, the other world grows larger too. For I can go far enough back to recollect and to thank the bright Sunday-school teacher, who, when we children had asked some unanswerable question, had the wit to stimulate our childish imaginings, by telling us that, when we came to heaven, we might ourselves talk with the actors in earth's eventful scenes, and that they then should tell us what we did not know. Noah should tell us of the flood; Romulus, how he built his walls; and Leonidas, of the defence of Thermopylæ. With the inquiring mind of a child, eager for more information, heaven is thus the home where he shall know everything. But time passed on, and the little sister, who was my playmate and companion, died of a sudden and went before me there. Then I saw, then I knew; this Bible taught me, if nothing else taught me, that when my turn came I should be with her. From that hour to this hour heaven has been to me the place of companionship. Knowledge? Yes, I suppose so. New senses? Yes. New senses not to be counted in place of these somewhat cumbrous five. But it is not such images which come first to him who has loved and who has said good-by. To that man heaven is—more and more as life goes on—the life where he is to be with him or her, her and him who have been the blessing of life here: from whom he has been parted, but whom he has not lost:

"For love is heaven, and heaven is love."

St. John, in Patmos, where his island was a prison, of which the ocean forged the chains, speaks of heaven in exultation, to say, "The sea is no more!" You must not quote that outburst of a prisoner to him who is just emancipated from his daily toil, and stands upon the sea-beach to look at the unbounded horizon for the first time in his life, and drink in some notion of eternity and infinity. To the prisoner heaven is freedom. To the wanderer it is his father's house. To the ignorant it is learning. To the bookworm it is simplicity. To this poor, lame boy, to that weak, deformed girl, it is the roving free through limitless existence. To the slave, worn under the lash, it is a world without labor. To the weary it is rest. To the sanguine it is action. To the doubtful it is truth. To the struggling it is peace. To the sick it is health. To him who is careworn, distressed, pulled hither and thither, with not a moment he can call his own, it is eternity; that is to say, it is life without time; where there are no minutes, no hours, no days, and no years; no late, no early, no tedious, no slow, no thought nor care for time.

Nor is it true that these conceptions of heaven weaken each other, because they thus contradict each other.

Those who are eager to find action in heaven need not fear but there will be motive enough, effort enough, in life which reaches from one side of eternity to the other. Duty there must be where there are God's children with their father. But,—this is the promise, that whether the faithful spirit, sent on some errand, pass from one end of heaven to the other, or whether he sit at the footstool, as those do who serve while they wait, there is no more wear and tear, no more fatigue for him. He shall "rest from his labors." And this is the promise all along; the spirit remains, but the limitation is gone. The mind could once be cramped by a fevered brain, or by paralyzed fingers; but now it is free! The soul may soar to the top wing-beat of its noblest aspirations, and never outwear itself in its effort; yet, it shall all the while be resting in its Father's smile. These pests of earth, fatigue, nervous exhaustion, unrest, with all the attendant despairs and melancholies,—powers of evil, as the poets well call them,—which may haunt us all the closer as our effort is the nobler, belong in this life; because this life means partnership of a finite body and an infinite soul. The soul starts in the morning on an angel's work; and the body, too,—has it not been made by an Almighty Hand?—boldly takes up the soul's instructions, bravely follows on hour after hour, till time tells. It quivers, wavers, faints, fails. Why not? How else? It is clay at best. Earth-made! And this poor soul inspires it as it can, fans its faintness as it can, cheers it as it can, braces it to the angel duty yet undone. As a hunted prince in the desert rubs down the legs of his failing steed, and bathes his mouth, the willing soul keeps the poor body up to the last. But they are yoked unequally; they are of different nature; and at last the poor body must fall back to sleep, to rest, to be recreated and recruited, beore, with another morning, it can begin again. The flying steed is yoked to an earthly roadster. He can inspirit him, but he cannot teach him to fly. This is the only fatigue a true man ought to know. For that other *ennui*, of the man who stands all day idle, no true man ought to know. You are worn down, because your plans are beyond the power of your engine. Driven even to its quickest, when you say you have but just begun, it has to stop till it can cool down. The heated metal must relax. The parts must take their old places before you can drive it again at full steam.

From such a life, so limited, hampered, thwarted, the infinite soul springs, at death, into the heaven where it is held in no such bondage. It may move forever on the swiftest wings,—side by side with God's own spiritual laws, woven in with them. It comprehends them. It works with them, unfettered now, and easy. It is not strange that that soul finds a heaven which is at once the home of rest and of duty!

I may speak, then, of contrasted pictures, without hazarding their possibility.

Return from these to the imaginations of the more devout poets, which till now I have passed by.

Here is the prayer of Festus, in the poem now forgotten. Like all the impure in heart, who would fain be pure, he cries:—

> "I could not look on Thee whate'er I was,
> So when we had winged through Thy wide world of things
> And seen stars made and saved, destroyed and judged,
> I said, and trembled lest Thou shouldst not hear me
> And make Thyself right ready to forgive,
> I *will see* God, before I die, in heaven."

And Dante, toiling on from that dark forest, where in middle life he was lost, led by sage to sage, from step to step, from saint to saint, even from world to world, finds heaven at last:—

> "When with close heed, suspense and motionless,
> Wondering I fixed so earnestly my ken
> On the everlasting splendor."

These pictures are drawn from the highest flights of faith. Their prototypes are in the gospels and in the epistles, where the pure in heart, as the crown of their eternal quest, *see God*.

It is only before the Spirit comes that James and John wish to sit, the one on the right hand and the other on the left of the Lord. In their later lives, the younger James says, "Be patient, brethren, until the coming of the Lord. Behold the husbandman waiteth for the precious fruit of the earth, being long patient over it, until it receive the early and latter rain." His heaven is a ripe fruit, which these showers and these suns have matured.

Peter's heaven is "An inheritance incorruptible, and that fadeth not away."

John whispers, or sings, "Beloved, now are we children of God, and it is not yet made manifest what we shall be. We know that if he shall be manifested we shall be like him; for we shall see him even as he is."

Paul, practical always and seeking some result, is "in a strait betwixt the two; having the desire to depart and to be with Christ, for it is very far better."

Stephen cries, "I see the heavens open, and a son of man stand at the right hand of God."

All of them drinking in something of the spirit of the Master: "I have a fire to be lighted, and how I wish that it were already kindled! I have a baptism to be baptized with, and how am I straitened till it be accomplished!" His heaven is looking from his Father's presence on a world warmed, lighted, and redeemed.

And here I have cited only one or two among the thousands upon thousands of imaginations of heaven with which Saviour, prophet, poet, and martyr would have supplied us. Among them all I may hardly more than once have struck the key-note for your idea of heaven or yours; for as on earth there are many homes, no two quite alike, so in heaven there are many homes, and no one the same as another. As between these earthly homes there is the quickest sympathy and the closest love, if only the kingdom of heaven is at hand; so between those myriad homes of that other life; and among them all there is one spirit, and they are made perfect in one! So is it that each soul of us here, for his own cheer, for his own help, for his own training, has, if he be faithful, pure, and wise, the idea or vision of heaven which for him is best at this moment. It is not for me to paint your picture, nor for you to paint mine. For it is thus that to you and me God is pleased to give one more stimulus for our upward way. When I lay me down to sleep, and pray God to take my soul if I die before the morning, it is not to any strange city, unknown to me and unknowable. The home that is offered me is the mansion for which I am ready, and the heaven which I vaguely dream of to-day is the heaven which shall be mine to-morrow.

And to any man who comes to me, and says that he has found no satisfactory conception of heaven, I should say that probably he has been seeking the image, instead of the reality. We cannot "imagine," we cannot clothe in images, that which our Lord himself did not choose to picture, to describe, to image, or to define. Let a man rather devote himself to making simpler his idea of God and of his own soul. Let him accustom himself to the thought, that, as his soul uses this body, so it may use other bodies of higher power, with senses we have not yet attained to; unlimited, indeed, in their range and sphere. What the limitations of earth are, we know, alas! too well. But yet we are able to conceive of God as free from these limitations. Nay, we free ourselves from them as we plan for our own future and set in order its activities. And here is the promise to you and to me: that what we need is ours. What we have gained is ours. For our labor, rest. For our hunger, food. For our thirst, the water of life. For our love, such love as Christ's; as all good angels'; as the very love of God. And no man is to fear that he is not ready for the place. What the Saviour went for was to prepare the place for him. What place I am fit for that place I find.

In my Father's house are many homes!

www.ingramcontent.com/pod-product-compliance
Lightning Source LLC
Chambersburg PA
CBHW020141170426
43199CB00010B/840